Christmas in America's Capital

Christmas in America's Capital

Christmas Around the World
From World Book

World Book, Inc.
a Scott Fetzer company
Chicago

Staff

Editor in Chief
Dale Jacobs

General Managing Editor, World Book Publishing
Paul A. Kobasa

Editorial

Managing Editor, General Publishing and Annuals
Maureen Mostyn Liebenson

Associate Editor
Shawn Brennan

Writers
Scott Thomas, Karen Zack Ingrebretsen

Manager, Digital Cartography
Wayne K. Pichler

Permissions Editor
Janet T. Peterson

Manager, Research Services
Loranne K. Shields

Art

Manager, Graphics and Design
Sandra Dyrlund

Senior Designer
Don Di Sante

Photographs Editor
Sylvia Ohlrich

Production and Administrative Assistant
John Whitney

Marketing

Director, Direct Marketing
Mark R. Willy

Marketing Analyst
Zofia Kulik

Production

Director, Manufacturing and Pre-Press
Carma Fazio

Manager, Manufacturing
Barbara Podczerwinski

Senior Production Manager
Madelyn Underwood

Print Promotional Manager
Marco Morales

Proofreader
Anne Dillon

Text Processing
Gwendolyn Johnson

World Book wishes to thank the following individuals for their contributions to ***Christmas in America's Capital:*** Claire Pritchett, White House Visitor's Office; Jan Clark, Public Programs Division, U.S. Botanic Gardens.

 This is a revised and retitled edition of a previously published work, *Christmas in Washington, D.C.*

World Book, Inc.
233 N. Michigan Avenue
Chicago, IL 60601

For information about other World Book publications, visit our Web site **http://www.worldbook.com,** or call **1-800-WORLDBK (967-5325).** For information about sales to schools and libraries, call **1-800-975-3250 (United States); 1-800-837-5365 (Canada).**

Library of Congress Cataloging-in-Publication Data

Christmas in America's capital.
p. cm. -- (Christmas around the world from World Book)
"This is a revised and retitled edition of a previously published work, Christmas in Washington, D.C."--T.p. verso.
ISBN 0-7166-0803-0
1. Christmas--Washington (D.C.) 2. Washington (D.C.)--Social life and customs. I. Christmas in Washington, D.C. II. Series.

GT4986.W37C433 2005
394.2663'09753--dc22

2004012805

Printed in the United States of America
1 2 3 4 5 6 7 8 9 10 09 08 07 06 05 04

Contents

A Capital Christmas

The ancient Romans had a minor god of gates and doors named Janus. His head featured two faces. One looked backward, and one looked forward. Washington is a Janus-faced kind of place. As the capital of the nation, it is immersed in history and tradition. And as the capital of the nation, it seethes with politics and the brokering of power. Tradition resists change; power thrives on it—one city, two faces. One looks

Christmas trees light up the North Portico of the White House at Christmastime.

backward, and one looks forward. But, if it is true that one needs to know the past to understand the future, then a nation's capital should have two faces.

In the United States, Christmas also has more than one face. It is, first of all, a sacred celebration of the birth of Christ. It is also a family celebration, an affirmation of kinship and home. And in the United States, Christmas is also something of a national holiday, complete with an economy and economic indicators. The varied faces of Christmas in America resist and embrace change. They must. While the essential nature and message of the Nativity of Jesus remains constant, the other celebrations change, exactly as the family and the nation change.

Georgetown University (left). *A statue on the campus* (below) *honors the founder John Carroll, who was the first Roman Catholic bishop in America.*

Christmas in Washington is a sacred celebration of the birth of Jesus; it is an affirmation of the family and home; but, above all, it is the story of a national celebration. A Christmas in Chicago is not very different from a Christmas in Atlanta or Boston or Sacramento. Christmas in Washington, however, is unique.

Officially, the government of the United States does not celebrate religious holidays. Unofficially, of course, it does. There is a national *Christmas tree; there is a* capitol *Christmas tree; there is a White House decked out for the holidays; there is Christmas on the National Mall, a holiday celebration not quite like any other in the world.*

Officially, the churches of Washington are exactly like churches in Chicago or Atlanta or Sacramento. Unofficially, certain churches in Washington are viewed as national institutions. And the celebration of the anniversary of the birth of Jesus in such a church is not quite like a Christmas service anywhere else.

College students, home for the holidays (below), *stroll across the West Capitol Grounds. Narrow Georgetown streets become snowbound after a holiday storm* (right). *One of the oldest communities in North America, Georgetown was a thriving tobacco trading port before becoming part of the District of Columbia. The west front of the Capitol as seen from a detail of the Grant Memorial* (far right). *The Memorial, which stretches for 252 feet along the foot of Capitol Hill, was dedicated in 1922.*

Washingtonians would agree that they share their city with the nation and the rest of the world. Thus, Christmas in their city is shared with the nation and the world. The National Christmas Tree is the nation's tree. Christmas at the White House is a symbol of Christmas at every American house. As we shall see, the National Mall is the nation's Main Street. And the Washington, or National, Cathedral, while an Episcopal church, is indeed a "house of prayer for all people."

Christmas in Washington

At one o'clock on the afternoon of December 7, 1941, Eleanor Roosevelt received luncheon guests at the White House. She announced that "the president would be unable to come down to luncheon." One of the guests, H. P. Hamlin, remembered that a flustered Mrs. Roosevelt had confided that "the news from Japan was very bad." At 9:30 the night before, the president had been called away from dinner to read intercepted telegrams that outlined Japan's formula for a "diplomatic Pacific settlement."

Franklin Delano Roosevelt addresses the nation, via radio, on Christmas Eve, 1941. To his right is British Prime Minister Winston Churchill. The first National Christmas Tree had just been lighted.

Directly above the Blue Room, where Mrs. Roosevelt was receiving, Franklin Roosevelt was eating lunch from a desktop tray in his study. At approximately 1:40 the telephone rang. Frank Knox, the secretary of the navy, had just received a radio message from Honolulu: "AIR RAID ON PEARL HARBOR THIS IS NOT A DRILL."

On Monday, December 8, Congress declared war on Japan. On December 11, Germany and Italy declared war on the United States. World War II had escalated to global proportions.

In those final days of 1941, tension filled the streets and offices of official Washington. Many believed the city would be bombed. A blackout was ordered. At the White House, a special detachment of military police was put on 24-hour duty. The military and the Secret Service demanded that additional measures be taken to protect the chief executive: machine guns on the White House roof; bullet-proof window glass; a sandbag barricade 15 feet high around the Executive Mansion and offices; a bomb shelter; and a White House repainted in standard Army Air Corps camouflage. Roosevelt balked at their demands. They also ordered that the Washington Community Christmas Tree, tra-

The National Christmas Tree, shown in 2002, is decorated differently each year by the General Electric Company. It is a living tree planted on the Ellipse, south of the White House. The Washington Monument is in the background.

ditionally located near the White House and lighted by the president, be suspended for the duration. If Roosevelt balked at the serious measures, he bristled over the Christmas tree ban.

As a master politician, Franklin Roosevelt well understood the value of symbols. We were fighting a war to preserve our heritage; Christmas was part of that heritage. Besides, the president loved Christmas and Christmas trees. He would have the tree. The Secret Service refused. Roosevelt retorted that their attitude smacked of cowardice. The tree, they argued, would interfere with the civil defense of the city. Roosevelt was adamant. The Secret Service offered a compromise; there could be a tree, but no lights.

In the end, there was a tree. There were lights. And President Roosevelt participated in the lighting ceremony. He even renamed the tree. The Washington Community Christmas Tree became the National Christmas Tree. He did compromise to the extent that the tree was moved from Lafayette Park, which was public, to the south lawn of the White House, which was private although highly visible.

On December 24, 1941, President and Mrs. Roosevelt stood under the great, curving south portico of the White House. Next to the president stood British Prime Minister Winston Churchill, who had arrived that morning amid great secrecy. Because of the blackout, they could not see the 15,000 people standing outside the iron fence surrounding the south lawn. The president pushed a button, which triggered a signal in a hole dug under the tree. Inside, an electrician threw a switch. And, suddenly, the tree was ablaze with thousands of lights. A kaleidoscope of color reflected across the facade of the old house and across the faces of the people. Spontaneously, they began to sing. Across the nation that Christmas Eve, millions of people listening over their radios heard Roosevelt and Churchill join in the caroling. Later, Churchill expressed to all Americans his comfort at sharing Christmas joys with them. But it was thoughts of children that inspired his message to Americans in 1941.

> . . . Let the children have their night of laughter . . . Let us grown-ups share . . . in their unstinted pleasures before we turn again to the stern tasks and the formidable years that lie before us, resolved that by our sacrifice and daring these same children shall not be robbed of their inheritance or denied their right to live in a free and decent world.

And so in the first fearful weeks of World World II, the National Christmas tree came to be. The idea, however, was conceived in 1923 by Frederick Feiker of the Society of Electrical Development, an organization promoting the use of electricity. Feiker convinced President Coolidge to participate in a tree-lighting ceremony. A large tree from Coolidge's native Vermont was erected on the Ellipse, a circular park that connects the White House to the Mall. Coolidge turned on the lights but, true to form, refused to speak.

The event was nearly canceled after a single year. In 1924, Coolidge protested the cutting of trees for Christmas. To save the Community Tree, Feiker arranged for a living tree to be planted on Sherman Square, east of the White House. Coolidge again participated in the lighting. This tree, however, did not live through the winter.

In Washington, politics permeates everything, including Christmas trees. While Feiker's Community Tree did become a tradition, it remained something of an orphan. It was, over the years, moved from the Ellipse, to Sherman Square, to Lafayette Park (north of the White House), to the south lawn, and back to the Ellipse. This shifting may have been due to politics—to pressures brought to bear on the president by conservation-minded citizens. When the nation was in a "conservation mood," a live tree was planted. The trouble with a permanent living tree was that it always died. This may have been bad luck or a matter of benign neglect. Washington, designed by Pierre L'Enfant in the late 1700's, is a city of formal squares and circles. A single, large evergreen does not well fit the character of L'Enfant's perfect little parks that circle the White House. Planting a tree to satisfy conservationists was easy enough; keeping it alive, however, was probably not much of a priority. When the next tree was planted, it was probably moved to a new spot in the hope that, if it did survive, it might look a little less out of place during the 51 weeks that it was not decorated for Christmas.

By 1941, when Roosevelt rechristened the tree, the idea of a living tree was given up. In times of war, conservation becomes a moot point. And certainly no one wanted a fir tree growing in the center of the south lawn.

In 1954, the National Christmas Tree was moved permanently

The Capitol Christmas Tree, supplied by the U.S. Forest Service, is erected on the Capitol's west front terraces and is visible the full length of the Mall.

to the Ellipse. That year community leaders organized the Pageant of Peace, which was intended to serve as a symbol of the country's goal for international peace. The pageant was scheduled to begin with the tree-lighting ceremony, which was moved forward by about a week at the request of President Eisenhower, who preferred to be home in Gettysburg before Christmas Eve. The Pageant of Peace, which continues today, includes nightly entertainment; a burning Yule log; a Nativity scene; and 56 eight-foot trees, representing the U.S. states and territories and the District of Columbia. The 56 smaller trees are decorated with ornaments donated by participating organizations, including children's museums, YMCAs, Girl Scout and Boy Scout councils, and church groups. All the ornaments are encased in plastic globes to shield them from harsh weather.

The Pageant of Peace inaugurated the era of giant National Christmas trees, which were annually donated by the different states. Each state, of course, vied to send a bigger and better tree. The record is held by Arizona, which, in 1965, sent a 99-foot-tall tree that was over a century old. But in 1972, renewed pressure from conservationists ended the era of "great" trees. The last huge cut tree was seen in 1972, which was about the time that "conservation" became known as "ecology." With the nation again interested in conservation, the National Tree was again a living tree. And, again, the living tree died. Even its replacement succumbed, having been blown over during a violent rainstorm. Finally, the National Park Service attacked the Christmas tree "problem." In 1978, after a determined search, a park ranger found the perfect tree—a 30-foot blue spruce growing in the yard of the Myers family of York, Pennsylvania. It had been Mrs. Myers's Mother's Day gift 15 years earlier. A price of $1,500 was negotiated. The tree was carefully uprooted, transported, and replanted on the Ellipse. It continues to thrive today and is now more than 40 feet tall. The permanent National Tree grows just east of the north entrance to the Ellipse and is part of a border of elms that frames this large, oval parade ground. Thus, the tree does not intrude upon the symmetry of L'Enfant's President's Park. One of the most carefully tended trees in the world, the National Christmas Tree should survive for generations and reach a height equal to those giant trees of the '50s and '60s.

Although the Park Service cares for the tree, the General Electric Company donates the lighting and design that will adorn the tree throughout the Christmas season. Each year a new theme is chosen.

A festive tree-lighting ceremony begins the Pageant of Peace each year. At the conclusion of the musical program, which often includes international celebrities, guest choruses, and Santa Claus

The National Christmas Tree glows with patriotic colors during the 2001 Christmas Pageant of Peace on the Ellipse. The White House is in the background.

himself, the president traditionally gives an annual holiday message and pushes the button lighting the tree. Throngs of tourists and Washingtonians gather on the Ellipse for the opening of the Pageant of Peace. The nightly programs are also well attended through New Year's Eve.

Over the years, there have been variations in the Pageant prompted by local or world events. In 1980, for instance, the National Christmas Tree was fully lighted for only 417 seconds—one second for each day the American hostages had been held captive in Iran. And on Christmas Eve of 1985, President Reagan directed that the lights on the tree be turned down momentarily in support of American hostages in Lebanon and their families at home.

In 2001, the tree was decorated in a patriotic theme, with red, white, and blue lights and stars. Assisting President Bush and the first lady in lighting the tree were two individuals who had lost family members in the terrorist attacks of September 11, 2001.

Another popular Christmas tree in Washington is the Capitol Christmas Tree, also known as "The People's Tree."

The tradition of displaying a Christmas tree on the Capitol grounds is relatively new. Correspondence of 1919 in the records of the Architect of the Capitol indicates that a tree was purchased that year. However, it was not until 1964 that a procedure was initiated and a Christmas tree-lighting ceremony established.

Each year White House employees put up Christmas decorations in the historic East Room.

In 1963, House Speaker John W. McCormack suggested to J. George Stewart, Architect of the Capitol, that a Christmas tree be placed on the Capitol grounds. A live 24-foot tree was planted on the west front lawn. In the years of 1964 through 1967, this tree was decorated and a tree-lighting ceremony held. Unfortunately, a combination of factors, including a severe windstorm in the spring of 1967, caused the tree to die in 1968. The 1968 Christmas tree was made from two white pines and was 30 feet tall. That year, a tradition was started. And since 1970, the U.S. Forest Service has provided the People's Tree, always obtaining it from one of the country's majestic national forests.

North of the National Christmas Tree stands the White House. Completed in 1800, it is the oldest public building in the District of Columbia. The only president who did not live in the house was George Washington, who personally approved architect James Hoban's plans. From early December through the end of the month, the White House is lavishly decorated for Christmas, featuring a different theme each year. The view of the White House from the Ellipse includes all of the south lawn, nearly 18 acres, and the south facade, graced by a col-

The President's Christmas Tree* (insert), *which is donated by the National Christmas Tree Association, is transported to the White House in a horse-drawn wagon. The East Room of the White House* (left) *is lavishly decorated for Christmas. Through the years this room, perhaps the most historic in the nation, has been the scene of every kind of event: weddings, funerals, state dinners for visiting royalty, and even sumo wrestling matches.

umned, three-story portico. Under the carriage lights on either side of the portico entrance stand two conical evergreens. Typically, evergreen roping drapes the porch railing and the Truman Balcony, as well as down the two curving staircases that connect the first floor with the south lawn. A wreath hangs at each of the three levels of the south portico. Through the curved panes of glass in the center window one can see the White House Christmas tree, which stands in the center of the Blue Room.

In the past, public tours of the White House were conducted during the day on Tuesdays through Saturdays. And special "candlelight tours" were offered in the evenings starting on December 26. However, those customs changed after the terrorist attacks that took place in the United States on September 11, 2001. All White House tours were suspended for a time, and after that, only very limited groups of people (schoolchildren, youth groups, members of the military, and veterans) were permitted to tour the building, and only during the day.

Americans still want to see how their president's home is decorated for the holidays, however. To satisfy the public's curiosity, a number of new opportunities have been developed. The first lady often hosts a Christmas tour of the White House that is televised on a network TV station. And HGTV, a cable channel, films the setup of the decorations as they are installed and airs the special throughout the month of December. In addition, the White House Visitor's Center displays a replica of the White House Christmas tree and features models of other decorations specially selected to depict the year's theme. The Center also hands out booklets about that year's theme and decorations. The White House Web site, www.whitehouse.gov, offers 360-degree tours of the public rooms, all decked out for Christmas, and often includes video and audio clips of the first lady and some of the White House staff members discussing the holiday decorations and observances.

What one sees in the East Garden Room may differ from year to year. The Reagans once included a cone-shaped tree made from pink and white poinsettias. The George W. Bush family once chose to display a tree with ornaments designed and contributed by each state. Along the colonnade, built on the foundations of a similar structure designed by Thomas Jefferson, evergreen wreaths hang in the windows. The way is lighted by white candles, which stand on teakwood candlesticks made by resident craftspeople. Also along the way is the retrospective exhibit of White House Christmas cards, dating back to the Eisenhower administration in 1953.

At the end of the colonnade is the ground floor corridor. Before 1902, this area contained kitchens, pantries, and the furnace and coal rooms. Overhead is a vaulted ceiling constructed of stone, which originally supported the house above.

During the War of 1812, the British burned the White House.

The White House crèche, or Nativity scene, is placed in a window alcove in the East Room. It is seen here from the Cross Hall, which this particular year was decorated with poinsettias and evergreen wreaths and festoons.

To save time and money during the reconstruction, the interior was rebuilt with wooden supports. (The original construction, supervised by George Washington, was all masonry and much superior.) Over the next 120 years, water pipes, gas lines, furnace flues, and electrical wiring were cut through timbers. In 1902, the house's principal staircase was removed to enlarge the State Dining Room. In the process, load bearing walls were removed; the weight of the unsupported load was then simply shifted to existing timbers. On top of this, in 1927, a third floor, partially constructed of concrete, was added.

By 1948, the White House was in danger of collapsing. In August of that year, a leg of Margaret Truman's piano crashed through the second floor, causing the ceiling below to fall. Between 1948 and 1952, the entire inner structure of the house was removed and rebuilt in steel and concrete. Subbasements were dug, and a considerable number of service rooms were added.

Truman insisted that as much of the old as possible be saved. Along the ground floor corridor are a number of rooms paneled in pine, which was salvaged from the timbers that once supported the old house. The walls of this hallway are hung with portraits of first ladies, which during an evening tour are lighted by candles.

A broad flight of stairs leads from the ground floor corridor to the first, or state, floor. At the top of the stairs, to the right is the East Room, the largest and most formal of the state rooms. A highlight of the view into the beautifully appointed East Room is the traditional White House crèche. It was made in Naples, Italy, in the late 1700's. Its 57 carved wood and terra-cotta figures are exquisite examples of Old World craftsmanship. The crèche was a gift to the White House and to the American people from Mrs. Charles Engelhart, Jr., of Far Hills, New Jersey, and has been displayed each year since 1967 as part of the holiday celebrations. A new tableau was first displayed in 1999. The figures, which range in height from 12 to 18 inches, depict the Holy Family, the three kings, their attendants, shepherds, angels, cherubs, and animals associated with the Nativity story.

Several grand trees add majesty to the East Room. The number of trees and their locations vary from year to year. The trees are lavishly adorned with colorful ornaments and lights. Garlands of mixed greenery are suspended by ribbons around the gilded mirrors, which reflect and endlessly multiply the images of candles set in cande-

labra, which rest on the four fireplace mantels.

The East Room, designed by Hoban as the "public audience room," has been the scene of an extraordinary variety of events: Abigail Adams hung her wash here because she thought it indelicate to expose the presidential linen to public scrutiny; Thomas Jefferson and Meriwether Lewis planned the exploration of the West in the room. Union troops were billeted here during the Civil War; Teddy Roosevelt's boys roller-skated across the parquet floor; their father staged sumo wrestling matches on it; daughters of Presidents U.S. Grant, Theodore Roosevelt, Woodrow Wilson, and Lyndon Johnson were married in the East Room; and seven presidents, including Abraham Lincoln, Franklin Delano Roosevelt, and John Kennedy, laid in state here. It is, perhaps, the most historic room in America.

To the west is the Green Room,

President and Mrs. Reagan **(above)** *decorate their Christmas tree in the second floor center hall, which is part of the private quarters of the White House. Members of the White House staff* **(right)** *decorate the North Entrance for Christmas. The year was 1938; the low ramp leading to the door accommodated President Roosevelt's wheelchair.*

A White House Christmas tree. To allow room for the almost 20-foot tree, the chandelier was removed from the center medallion of the Blue Room.

a formal parlor used for small teas and receptions, with furniture in the style of the Federal period. Throughout the year, the renowned portrait of Benjamin Franklin by David Martin, which hangs above the fireplace, is a focal point of this traditional room. The room is lighted by candles set on various side tables and on the white marble mantel, which was purchased by President Monroe in 1817. Opposite the fireplace is an arrangement of two armchairs, a settee, and a drop-leaf table, all attributed to the American cabinetmaker Duncan Phyfe. On the table are two candles set in silver sticks that were used in this room by Dolley Madison. Between the candles is a silver-plated coffee urn that was owned by John Adams, who considered it one of his "most prized possessions."

During the holidays, the mantel becomes the focus of the Green Room. Again, the specific decorations change from year to year, usually depending on the chosen theme. In one year, following the theme of "Santa's Village," the mantel featured a handcrafted mantelpiece that depicted a night-time scene in Santa's Village, with elves and Mrs. Claus making sure all was ready for Santa's journey around the world.

Thomas Jefferson used the Green Room for dining. In the spirit of democracy, he insisted upon a round table so there would be no head, and he banished all servants during meals. Food and service dishes were placed in warming cabinets from which the president and his guests took turns serving. The resulting privacy and informality promoted frank and lively conversation, which Jefferson, who understood the isolation of the presidency, appreciated.

Beyond the Green Room is the Blue Room, which is "elliptical" or oval in shape. Presidents have traditionally used the room to receive guests. By tradition, the Blue Room is the residence of the official White House tree. The

The White House State Dining Room is decorated for Christmas with evergreen roping and poinsettias. The Healy portrait of Lincoln hangs above a mantel. The mantel is a copy of one originally installed during the Theodore Roosevelt administration. The original mantel was lost during the Truman renovation but reproduced at President Kennedy's suggestion.

A Civil War-era political cartoon shows President Lincoln offering Christmas dinner to reluctant guests. The empty chairs represent the Confederate States that have left the Union.

crystal chandelier is removed to make way for the tree, which usually stands almost 20 feet high. The tree is decorated with lights and a variety of ornaments, which change from year to year, but always follow a designated theme. Also, by tradition, the first family invites special groups and individuals to donate ornaments for the official tree. For example, one tree during the Kennedy administration was a "children's tree," with trimmings derived from the "Nutcracker Suite" ballet by Tchaikovsky, gingerbread cookies, tiny toys, wrapped packages, and straw ornaments, all made by blind or elderly craftspeople throughout the country. One of the Nixons' trees took its theme from two White House collection paintings by Severin Roesen—*Nature's Bounty* and *Still Life with Fruit*. The tree was filled with 3,000 satin-finish balls in gold, pink, red, blue, and green. A Clinton tree followed the theme of "The Twelve Days of Christmas," with 2,000 ornaments created by American art students. And the 2002 Bush tree illustrated the theme "All Creatures Great and Small," devoted to animals, including the companion animals that have graced the White House over its long life.

Each year the White House tree is donated to the president by the National Christmas Tree Association's champion grower. It is ceremoniously transported to the White House on a horse-drawn wagon.

The Blue Room is decorated in the Empire style popular when the house was rebuilt after the fire of 1814. At that time, President Monroe ordered new furnishings for the Executive Mansion. Included in this purchase were 38 pieces of gilded furniture made by Bellangé of Paris. This suite remained in the Blue Room until 1860, when President Buchanan's niece, Harriet Lane, sold it at auction. In 1902, Charles McKim, architect for the Roosevelt restoration, reproduced the Bellangé suite from photographs and a painting. In 1961, an original Bellangé chair was found and acquired by the White House. Since then a sofa and six more chairs have been returned to the house. Today, the Blue Room is furnished with a combination of the originals and the 1902 reproductions. Traditionally, a round table has been placed in the center of the room. Using the round table as protection, the president stood to one side of it to avoid being crushed during large, public receptions. Until 1930, the president received and shook hands with literally thousands of people on New Year's Day.

Next is the Red Room, a formal parlor of the American Empire period (1810-1830). The walls are hung with red twill satin, trimmed at the cornice and chair rail with a red and gold border. The furniture is American Empire upholstered in red and gold silk.

For Christmas, the Red Room is decorated differently each year, again depending on the chosen theme.

The Red Room was used by Dolley Madison for her popular Wednesday evening receptions. A painting of her hangs in the room. Abraham and Mary Lincoln also frequently used the Red Room for informal entertaining. A contemporary noted that it was furnished and decorated with pieces "very ancient, being bought or presented during Monroe's and Madison's administrations." The fireplace mantel is one of those "very ancient" pieces.

The Red Room opens directly into the State Dining Room, the setting for the White House's most elegant entertaining. This room is always spectacularly decorated for the holiday season.

One of the most popular White House decorations is showcased in the State Dining Room. It is the traditional gingerbread house, which is always expertly designed and crafted by the White House pastry chef. Each year the gingerbread house is unique, but it always demonstrates the chef's mastery of this Christmas culinary art. The 2001 gingerbread house was a replica of the White House as it looked in the 1800's. Illustrating the theme "Home for the Holidays," this house even featured models of the Bush family's two pet dogs romping in the snow outside the house.

Above the dining room fireplace hangs the famous George P. Healy portrait of Abraham Lincoln. The frame of Healy's portrait is draped with an immense garland trimmed with long, colorful ribbons. The mantel, embellished with ornamental plaster buffalo heads, is a reproduction of one installed by Theodore Roosevelt in 1902. During the Truman renovation, the original was removed and lost. In 1962, President Kennedy suggested that a copy of the buffalo mantel be re-installed. Carved into the mantel is an inscription written by John Adams on his second night in the Executive Mansion: "I pray Heaven to Bestow the Best of Blessings on THIS HOUSE and on All that shall hereafter Inhabit it. May none but Honest and Wise Men ever rule under this Roof."

First Lady Laura Bush shows off the White House gingerbread house, a replica of the White House in the 1800's. The house was made with 80 pounds of gingerbread, 30 pounds of chocolate, and 20 pounds of marzipan.

The Cross Hall is separated from the Entrance Hall by a colonnade of paired marble columns. Beyond it, garlands trimmed with ribbons are hung over the pier mirrors that reflect the grand staircase on the other side of the hall. Also in the Grand Foyer are four trees decorated with lovely ornaments such as ribbon roses, glass pine cones, and red balls.

In the East Wing is displayed a menorah. The White House menorah was designed and created by Mayrim Baram, a father who lost his young son during the 1973 Arab-Israeli War. In this menorah, Mr. Baram captures the horrors of war and expresses his hope for peace.

The White House is a unique place, neither private house nor public office. Throughout its history, it has continually changed, reflecting the changing character of the nation. Between 1800 and 1860, when the nation was primarily agrarian, the White House was something of a grand country house. Christmas celebrations in the Executive Mansion have also reflected the changing times and the people who lived through those times.

The first presidents were either Virginians or New Englanders. Most Virginians, due to their English and Anglican heritage, celebrated Christmas with feasting and revelry characteristic of old, feudal traditions. We know that one Christmas at Mount Vernon was celebrated with dancing, games, and a great feast that included five kinds of meat—beef, turkey, veal, duck, and ham; vegetables and several kinds of fruits and nuts; and desserts such as sweet potato pudding and plum pudding, served with jellies; the meal was washed down with wines and whiskey punches. It's likely that the young men continued to celebrate by stepping outside to shoot off their muskets. That, too, was a traditional part of the day.

President Grant receives King Kalakaua of the Hawaiian Islands at a Christmas reception. The drawing accurately depicts the East Room as remodeled by President and Mrs. Grant in what has since been described as "steamboat gothic."

The first inhabitants of the President's House were not, however, the Washingtons, but the Adamses, New Englanders of Puritan stock. The Puritans, a sect that grew out of the English Reformation, viewed Christmas with some suspicion. To them, holiday feasting and merrymaking seemed inappropriate, if not downright pagan. In certain New England colonies, Christmas was even banned by law. Christmas for the Adamses was likely more staid and reserved than a Christmas celebrated by the Virginian presidents.

The first Christmas celebration in the White House was a party held, in 1800, for the Adamses' granddaughter, 4-year-old Susanna. The Adamses had only moved in a month before. The rooms, largely unfinished, were cold, damp, and drafty. The only source of warmth was the fireplaces, which were numerous but incapable of warming the immense, high-ceilinged rooms. Mrs. Adams burned 20 cords of wood in each fireplace in an attempt to dry out the drafty house before that Christmas. Still, most guests, who were unable to conceal their discomfort, left early. (The Adamses were also considered somewhat chilly hosts.) While the children did not seem to mind the cold, the party was not altogether a success. Susanna bit the nose from a playmate's new wax doll after the envious playmate had smashed her new doll dishes. The president had to mediate a peace.

Thomas Jefferson also loved having his six grandchildren at the White House. One Christmas he held a party for them and 100 friends. A widower, Jefferson asked Dolley Madison to act as hostess. Unlike Abigail Adams, Mrs. Madison loved to entertain. There is no record that guests left early. Before it was over, Jefferson put his pet bird through its repertoire of tricks and played the violin while the children danced.

Mrs. Madison, as first lady, also hosted the first truly grand Christmas party at the White House. One of the guests was writer Washington Irving, who later noted that Dolley wore a bright purple dress, pearls, many bracelets, and the feathered turban that was her trademark. The State Dining Room was lighted by over 100 candles, and there was a waiter, probably a rented slave, for each guest. After dinner, the indomitable Mrs. Madison managed to charm her guests, many of whom were political enemies, into playing games, singing, and dancing.

Through the center window is the White House Christmas tree. Directly above is the oval room where Franklin Pierce probably placed the White House's first tree.

A late 1880's engraving shows guests arriving for a Christmas reception. Carriages drove through the portico. The lamps on the columns and ornamental fence, installed in 1833, were removed during the 1902 renovation.

President Hoover lights the Washington Community Christmas Tree in 1931. Mrs. Hoover and the President's grandchildren stand to his right.

President Andrew Jackson, also a widower, disliked being alone. Living with him were Jack and Emily Donelson, his beloved wife Rachel's niece and nephew, and their children. To entertain the children, Jackson invited 100 young Washingtonians for a Christmas "frolic in the East Room." After a supper, a great pyramid of decorated snowballs was dismantled from the center of the dining table and passed out to the children. Led by the president, the youngsters marched back into the East Room for a snowball fight. As each ball of starch-coated cotton sailed across the room and struck its target, it broke open, showering snow and candy kisses over little heads.

One Christmas morning, President Jackson woke to find a filled stocking hanging from the fireplace mantel. "Old Hickory" openly wept as he examined the contents, gifts and trinkets left by his adopted family. Jackson had been an orphan. As a child, he had never received a gift, nor even known that such a day as Christmas existed. Each Christmas, Jackson carried gifts and treats to orphanages in and around Washington. He stated that it was important "to begin our holiday by remembering the little ones who have no mothers or fathers to brighten life for them."

The first Christmas tree in the White House was decorated by Franklin Pierce in 1853. Pierce may have been trying to cheer his wife Jane, who became a recluse after the death of her only child. The boy died when the train carrying the president-elect and his family to Washington derailed. In 1853 the Christmas tree was a novelty in this country. The custom was brought to America by German immigrants, perhaps as early as the 18th century; it did not gain wide acceptance, however, until Godey's Lady's Book, in 1850, published an engraving of Queen Victoria's tree at Buckingham Palace. The first White House tree was probably a small evergreen placed on a table in one of the second floor parlors.

It is not known if the Lincolns had a Christmas tree in the White House. It is known, how-

The Franklin Delano Roosevelt family pose for a Christmas portrait in the East Room. The Roosevelts' family tree, which was upstairs in the private quarters, was always lighted with candles, because Eleanor and Franklin liked the "smell of hot evergreen."

ever, that on Christmas Day 1864, Tad Lincoln invited a gang of street urchins into the White House kitchen for dinner. When the appalled cook refused to feed them, Tad ran to his father. Although busy with guests, President Lincoln followed the boy downstairs to the kitchen and ordered the cook to serve the boys turkey dinners.

It was not unusual for Tad Lincoln to beg his father's intervention. (Everyone in the White House, except President and Mrs. Lincoln, thought Tad overindulged.) During an earlier Christmas season, he interrupted a Cabinet meeting when he discovered that a turkey, which he considered his pet, was going to be killed for the president's Christmas dinner. Passionately insisting that "Jack" was a good turkey, Tad implored his father to pardon the bird. Lincoln, who could deny Tad nothing, relented, and "Jack" became a familiar sight parading around the south lawn.

The next recorded appearance of a White House Christmas tree was in 1889. President and Mrs. Harrison staged a tree-trimming party that included their children, grandchildren, and the White House staff, all of whom received gifts. The tree was placed in the second floor, oval library. In 1895, President Cleveland had his White House tree wired for electric lights by an electrician, an operation performed that cost as much as a dollar a bulb. A tree in the White House became a tradition—that is, until Teddy Roosevelt became president.

Theodore Roosevelt, a staunch conservationist, decided that American forests were threatened by the cutting of trees for Christmas. To set an example, he forbade a tree in the White House. His sons, Archie and Quentin, however, smuggled one upstairs and hid it in their bedroom closet. On Christmas morning, the boys marched the family into their room, unveiled the tree, and offered everyone a gift. The president was not amused. After the holiday, the boys were sent to Gifford Pinchot, the country's foremost conservationist, to learn a lesson. The president's scheme backfired when Pinchot announced that the prudent cutting of smaller trees for Christmas could actually be helpful to the growth of forests. Pinchot and the National Forest Service also used the occasion to publicize the idea that growing Christmas trees might be a good way for farmers to utilize otherwise untillable land. But Roosevelt, on principle, continued to ban White House Christmas trees, while ignoring his sons' "closet" trees.

President Coolidge, who began the tradition of lighting what became the National Christmas Tree, also initiated the singing of carols under the north portico of the White House. In 1923, the choir of the First Congregational Church was invited by Mrs. Coolidge to sing carols following the Christmas Eve tree-lighting ceremony. The public was admitted to the north grounds and encouraged to sing along. Several days before the ceremony, the lyrics had been printed in the newspaper with the suggestion that they be brought, along with a flashlight. Separated from the tree-lighting ceremony, the carol sing-along had been practiced irregularly since the days of Coolidge. Lady Bird Johnson, in particular, encouraged it. It no longer occurs today.

The most exciting Christmas Eve in White House history was probably December 24, 1929. During a party for the Hoovers' grandchildren, it was discovered that the West Wing was on fire. All the men quietly excused themselves and rushed to the fire. Under the president's direction, papers, files, books, paintings, and even office furniture were saved from the flames that eventually gutted the office wing. No one was hurt, not even a puppy that was hidden in one of the offices. It was the president who remembered and ordered the rescue of the dog, which was a Christmas gift for an aide's son. Meanwhile, Mrs. Hoover kept the party going, calmly moving the children to the Christmas tree where she engaged them with stories.

As planned, the Hoovers hosted a dinner for 50 guests the following day. Each place at the table was set with either a bell or a brass candlestick. After dinner, President Hoover and his granddaughter led the guests on a march through the darkened parlors on the state floor. The men

The Harry Truman family celebrate Christmas in Blair House while the White House was being rebuilt. The Trumans moved into a White House in such bad shape that a leg of Margaret Truman's piano crashed through the floor.

carried the candles, the ladies rang the bells, and everyone sang carols.

Of all the first families that have lived in the White House, probably none have enjoyed Christmas more than the Franklin Roosevelts. Henrietta Nesbitt, the family's long-time cook and housekeeper, claimed that it was Eleanor Roosevelt's favorite time of the year, "when she seemed most happy." The first lady enjoyed shopping and searching for Christmas gifts throughout the year. She loved finding the perfect present for everyone, and she bought gifts for an extraordinary number of people—family, friends, her staff, the president's staff, the White House staff, even the house plumbers, electricians, and policemen. From year to year she kept running lists so that no gifts were repeated two years in a row. In October of each year, she took over a storage room on the third floor as her "toy room." Here, she stockpiled and eventually wrapped all the gifts. On the Sunday nearest to Christmas, the President and Mrs. Roosevelt personally greeted staff members and their families and passed out gifts from under a huge tree set in the East Room.

The East Room tree, which was constantly pushed into or out of an alcove to accommodate Mrs. Roosevelt's various Christmas activities, was lighted with electric bulbs. But the family tree, upstairs, was lighted with candles. Both the president and first lady claimed that Christmas was not Christmas without "the smell of hot evergreen." The fire marshall protested, but the president had his own way. Both Eleanor and Franklin insisted that Christmas in "this home away from home" must conform to Hyde Park traditions. Everything was done as it had always been done, and every year after Christmas Eve dinner, four generations

President and Mrs. Eisenhower* (above) *are surrounded by family and friends during Christmas dinner in the State Dining Room. Mamie Eisenhower so loved to decorate that she once put up 26 trees. A collection of White House Christmas cards* (below) *is displayed on the ground floor corridor during the holidays. Official White House Christmas cards were first mailed during the Eisenhower administration.

gathered around the fire in the president's oval study to listen to FDR read Dickens's *A Christmas Carol.* He knew most of it by heart and, over the years, worked up an "interpretation" that included a series of frightening ghosts.

Mamie Eisenhower staged some of the most spectacular Christmases that have ever taken place in the White House. As a couple, the Eisenhowers lived longer in the White House than in any other house; to Mamie Eisenhower, the White House was home. She also "simply loved to decorate." In 1959, she scattered 26 trees through the house, including one in the laundry. She had loudspeakers rigged up in the East Room, from which carols could be heard throughout the house. And she surrounded her-

Christmas parties are a White House tradition that dates back to 1800. John and Abigail Adams held a children's party for their granddaughter Susanna. President and Mrs. Clinton (left) *host a children's party in the East Room. Mrs. Kennedy* (insert) *shows children the White House tree in the Blue Room. Mrs. Kennedy also gave White House Christmas parties for handicapped children.*

self with friends and family, especially grandchildren, during the holidays. Like Mrs. Roosevelt, Mrs. Eisenhower's favorite time of the year was Christmas.

Aside from the family celebrations that take place during the Christmas holidays, there are many official gatherings and parties planned each year. At one time, parties for the sons and daughters of diplomats were held. More than 350 children would attend. The guests represented more than 75 countries, and many of the children came attired in native costumes.

There was also once a customary party for the children of White House staff members. First Lady Jacqueline Kennedy held a Christmas party for disadvantaged children—following a tradition that dated back to Jackson and, of course, to little Tad Lincoln.

In recent years, the president and first lady have invited a group of about 75 children to the White House for a special story hour. The president himself reads "A Visit from St. Nicholas," and the children chime in with whatever lines they know by heart.

Of course, children are not the only guests at White House Christmas events. Mrs. Gerald Ford once commented that the holidays seemed to be a season of "continual parties." President and Mrs. Ford, who loved to dance, hosted "an honest-to-goodness ball" in the Blue Room.

Although the Jimmy Carter family always returned to Plains, Georgia, for Christmas, they made certain to wish their staff and members of Congress a joyous holiday season. In the weeks before Christmas, the Carters hosted as many as 15 parties, including a grand Christmas ball for the members of Congress and

President Johnson and Lady Bird Johnson entertain Ludwig Erhard, chancellor of the former West Germany, with Christmas carols on the south portico—a White House tradition begun by Grace Coolidge.

their spouses—1,000 guests in all. It was fortunate that President Truman had had the floors reinforced with steel and concrete.

When the White House was reopened after the 1948-1952 renovations, many people, including Eleanor Roosevelt, felt that the rich patina of age, of history, had been wiped away. It was all too clean, too perfect. President Truman, who took great pride in the house, was perhaps stung by their words. While retaining as much of the old as possible, he had rebuilt the house to last for centuries—time enough for the house to again acquire the patina of times past. Those who are lucky enough to see the White House at Christmastime—either in person or via television or the Internet—are witnesses to that richness of history.

In the days before World War II, Washington was thought by many to be a provincial kind of place,

more like a sleepy, southern town than a world capital. Temporary residents bemoaned the lack of culture, and embassy officials, especially Europeans, considered Washington a "hardship posting." These attitudes have, of course, changed. As the United States became a world power, its capital became the center of that power; a place that attracted, rather than repelled. And as the city became more important internationally, its cultural life blossomed. The Smithsonian grew until its combined facilities were internationally recognized as one of the world's finest museum complexes. In 1971, the John F. Kennedy Center for the Performing Arts opened its doors, at once making Washington an important center for theater, opera, film, and symphonic music.

At Christmastime, activity at the Kennedy Center is intense; programs are extraordinary in quality, variety, and number. Each year the National Symphony performs Handel's *Messiah*, and the Choral Arts Society of Washington performs seasonal music from a variety of periods. This concert concludes with the audience joining the chorus in the singing of familiar carols, all accompanied by the house's magnificent organ.

Another sing-along at the Kennedy Center joins an audience of 2,700 people, a professional cho-

The Shiloh Choir entertains Washington office workers with holiday carols in the courtyard of the old Pension Building. From 1885 to 1926, payments to Civil War veterans went out from the offices along the galleries open to the courtyard. Today, the structure houses the National Building Museum and is open to the public.

ral group, and an orchestra for a mass rendition of the *Messiah*. People queue up for the free "Sing-Along Messiah" tickets early in the morning, as all seats are generally taken within 30 minutes of the opening of the box office.

The Kennedy Center also offers other free holiday performances that celebrate all the holidays of this time of year—Christmas, Kwanzaa, and Hanukkah. These take place in the Grand Foyer, where people can come and go as they please. Usually 200 to 300 people join each event.

A most unusual event is the "Tuba Christmas." Because of the presence of the many U.S. service bands, Washington has perhaps the nation's highest concentration of tuba players. For years they have gathered at Christmastime to delight listeners with holiday music in the low register. Any tuba player, amateur as well as professional, may participate.

On Christmas Eve, the Kennedy Center is the scene of another annual event: a live radio broadcast, hosted by a local radio station, that features a wide assortment of local musical entertainment. The program is free, and members of the audience are free to come and go at will.

While many traveling troupes have performed Tchaikovsky's *The Nutcracker*, Washington natives are partial to their own ballet company's production. Presented since 1961 at the Lisner Auditorium, *The Nutcracker* has become for many families a tradition that now spans several generations.

While the Kennedy Center offers the widest variety of holiday programs, Christmas events are presented all over the city—in churches, private homes, and even office buildings. At Constitution Hall, U.S. Army and Navy bands offer special concerts. At the Capital Children's Museum, a number of Christmas programs and workshops take place. Children might make their own wrapping paper, make New Year's party hats, do a Kwanzaa craft, or write a resolution on the New Years' Resolution Wall at the museum.

Washington is a city where history and tradition are omnipresent. As a result, old buildings generally do not get torn down. They languish for a generation or two while committees debate their merit, both historic and artistic. A new generation then "discovers" and restores the old, utilizing their spaces in ways never dreamed of by the builders. Thus, the old Pension Building became the National Building Museum. Its immense atrium, which once housed files on Civil War veterans, now provides a kind of all-purpose space where, during the holidays, musical programs are presented for the enjoyment of office workers. The Old Post Office, a huge, Victorian pile on Pennsylvania Avenue that was, for three generations, considered an eyesore, has become a shopping mall, as well as home to some of the city's liveliest night-spots. Here, each Christmas season, musicians, jugglers, and singing toy soldiers entertain shoppers. Another landmark, Georgetown's Old Stone House (the oldest house in Washington, buit in 1765), is now the scene of annual Christmas chamber concerts.

One of the city's most beloved Christmas traditions is played out in what is, perhaps, the city's

Attending a performance of Tchaikovsky's **The Nutcracker** *at George Washington University's Lisner Auditorium has become a traditional outing for many Washington families.*

Dickens's **A Christmas Carol** *is presented each December at Ford's Theatre, which was closed the night Lincoln was assassinated and was not reopened, as a theater, for 103 years.*

strangest and most tragic building. Dickens's classic *A Christmas Carol*, a story of bitterness, ghosts, and spiritual redemption, is presented annually at Ford's Theatre, a place of both bitterness and renewal.

Originally a Baptist church, the building was completed in 1839, four years before the publication of *A Christmas Carol*. In 1861, the church was remodeled into an opera house. It burned in 1862 and was, in 1863, rebuilt as a theater. On the night of April 14, 1865, John Wilkes Booth stole into the presidential box during a presentation of *Our American Cousin*, a play solely remembered for this one night's production. Using a derringer, Booth shot Abraham Lincoln and dramatically leaped onto the stage, breaking his leg in the process. In the wake of this tragedy, Ford's Theatre closed, seemingly forever.

During the 1870's, the building was converted into government offices. In June of 1893, the interior collapsed; 22 people were killed; 68 more were injured. Haunted by tragedy, the building was again closed. It sat empty for nearly another 40 years.

In 1932, Ford's Theatre reopened as a museum, housing the famous Oldroyd collection of Lincolniana. Among the relics were the flag and the spur that caused Booth to break his leg, as well as fragments of Lincoln's clothing snatched as he lay wounded in the theater.

On the eve of the centennial of Lincoln's death, Congress appropriated funds to restore Ford's

Theatre. The restoration, based upon Mathew Brady photographs taken the day Lincoln died, was so authentic it was decided that the building should be reopened as a theater. On Lincoln's Birthday, 1968, the first new production since *Our American Cousin* was staged in Ford's Theatre. A production of *A Christmas Carol* was first offered the following December.

So, after 103 years, the strange story of Ford's Theatre came full circle; audiences again watched actors play upon that stage; and audiences once again strained to see beyond the draperies into the shadows of that box just above and to the right of the apron. It is a fitting place for Dickens's tale of a past that haunts the present as well as the future.

In most American cities, the term Christmas on the mall

A craftsman demonstrates the making of nutcrackers at the Smithsonian's National Museum of American History.

might be mistaken for Christmas *at* the mall, a term that conjures up images of scowling shoppers marching, bags in hand, under decorated fir trees to the beat of canned Christmas carols. Of course, Washington, like every major American city, has its suburbs, which like all suburbs, are served by shopping malls. But in Washington the "mall" is not a shopping center. The "mall" is the National Mall, a very broad alley of grass bordered by ordered rows of trees and lined on both sides by immense and grand public buildings. Officially, the National Mall is 14 blocks long. Unofficially, it stretches more than 23 blocks from the Capitol to the Lincoln Memorial and the Potomac River beyond. It is, unquestionably, one of the great urban spaces of the world.

Christmas decorations adorn the inside of the Smithsonian's Arts Industries Building in Washington, D.C.

The name *National Mall* offers a clue to the function of this immense space. It is a "national" place as opposed to a local one. If the city of Washington has such a thing as a "Main Street," it is Pennsylvania Avenue, not the Mall. On a local level, the National Mall is a kind of backyard, handsome and useful, but not exactly the center of things. It is a space that makes sense only as a symbol, a kind of national main street, central park, and cultural center rolled into one. Along its borders are the Capitol, the White House (via the Ellipse), and the nation's public record and vision of itself: the National Archives, the monuments and memorials to its national heroes. Here too are nine museums of the Smithsonian complex.

When Pierre L'Enfant planned Washington, he included, where the Mall is now situated, a "Grand Avenue, 400 feet in breadth, and about a mile in length." He envisioned that it would be lined with "spacious houses and gardens, such as may accommodate foreign ministers." L'Enfant did not envision a national cultural center. The Mall as we know it today was not part of L'Enfant's original plan of Washington.

By 1848, when the cornerstone of the Washington Monument was laid, L'Enfant's plan for the city was considered dated and unimportant. By the early 1850's his Grand Avenue had become overgrown in the fashion of the romantic school of English landscaping. It was at approximately this time that the word *mall* was first used to describe this space. The word is derived from the old French word *mail* or *maul,* which means mallet. A maul was used in the playing of the 17th-century game, pall-mall pronounced *pell mell*, which can be loosely translated as ball mallet or hammer ball. The game consisted of hitting a ball through a circle at the end of a grassy alley. When the game went out of fashion, European cities were left with pall-mall alleys, which eventually became walkways, carriage drives, or bridle paths (the most famous of which was London's). Thus, in England, a grassy, shaded walk, or promenade, became known as a "mall." When English landscaping spread to America, English terminology spread with it.

The first step toward turning Washington's mall into a National Mall was unintentionally taken in 1855 when Congress authorized the construction of the Smithsonian Institution in that romantically overgrown park; the park also contained a singularly unhealthy swamp, the remnants of an old canal, and a railroad line and station. The "mall" remained in this condition until the early 1900's.

In 1893, millions of Americans visited the Columbian Exposition in Chicago, an early world's fair. What people saw and the images they took home changed the faces of cities and towns all over the country. The designers of the fair had, for the most part, been trained at the *École des Beaux-Arts* in Paris. They returned home to America imbued with ideals of the Beaux Arts. And on the lakefront in Chicago they erected the "white city," which to the majority of Americans who had never been to Europe looked like a vision of Imperial Rome. It was planned, ordered, fairly restrained, and grandiose in scale. People went home, looked around, and decided something was missing. Washingtonians, including con-

Thousands of tiny white lights sparkle in the trees outside a restaurant near Washington Harbor, a short ride from the Mall.

One of the Christmas trees at the National Museum of American History is displayed next to Horatio Greenough's statue of George Washington in a Roman toga. Commissioned by Congress in the 1850's, the statue caused enormous trouble. Intended for the center of the Capitol rotunda, it was deemed inappropriate for that august spot, which has remained empty. It was eventually placed out on the west lawn. However, a half-naked George Washington left out in the snow seemed to give everyone the shivers. The statue, which cost the then-enormous sum of $45,000, was too valuable to destroy. So, Congress, long ago, sent the statue to the Smithsonian in the hope that it would quietly disappear.

gressmen, were no exception. They looked around, decided something was missing, and started a committee, which was peopled by the same artists and architects who planned the Chicago exposition. The result was and is, modern-day Washington, including the National Mall—that symbolic main street of the nation.

Christmas on the Mall is, thus, more than Christmas in Washington. It is, like all events on the Mall, national, rather than local, in character—a symbol of how we view ourselves as a nation. Officially, the government of the United States does not celebrate Christmas. Unofficially, it does. The National Christmas Tree and the highly decorated White House testify to the fact. And up and down the length of the Mall stand the various publically funded museums that make up the Smithsonian complex; most sponsor holiday programs and exhibitions, which annually draw immense crowds from around the nation and world. Although always a busy place, the Mall has, in fact, two big tourist seasons: summertime and Christmas.

Without the special programs, the Christmas decorations along the Mall would still draw tourists and Washingtonians. Both the National Christmas Tree and the Capitol Tree can be viewed from up and down and across the Mall's great vistas. The south facade of the White House, lighted for Christmas, can also be seen, via the Ellipse, from the unofficial, western section of the National Mall. Many of the Mall's public buildings are extravagantly decorated for the season; for example, the old Smithsonian Building, that fanciful, castlelike structure that sticks out onto the Mall, is usually festooned with evergreen garlands. The Library of Congress, which is just up Capitol Hill, has a spectacular Christmas tree. After years of bringing in an immense 30-foot-tall natural tree through the 6-foot-wide doors of the Library, the staff decided to switch to an 18-foot artificial tree. Although not as big as the natural trees of the past, this tree still requires many members of the grounds crew to put it together and decorate it. Adjacent to the Library of Congress is the Folger Shakespeare Library. And for one weekend every December, the Library celebrates the holidays as they would have been enjoyed long ago.

The Folger Shakespeare Library is an independent research library. Opened in 1932, it was a gift to the American people from Henry Clay Folger and his wife Emily Jordan Folger. A major center for scholarly research, the Folger houses the world's largest collection of Shakespeare's printed works, in addition to a magnificent collection of other rare Renaissance books and manuscripts on all disciplines—history and politics, theology and exploration, law and the arts. The collection consists of approximately 310,000 books and manuscripts; 27,000 paintings, drawings, engravings, and prints; and musical instruments, costumes, and films.

The Folger is also a lively center for the literary and performing arts. Evidence of this is the Folger Consort, which presents music from the 1100's through the 1700's and is recognized as a model chamber music residency. And it is the Consort that hosts a holiday concert at the Library in December. One year, the Consort performed "A Canterbury Christmas." In the festively decorated Elizabethan Theatre, the Consort, with a guest soprano and a choir of boys, presented an all-English Christmas program, filled with the sweetness and liveliness that made English music a model all over late-medieval Europe. In addition to yuletide sacred music, the Consort performed pieces in honor of St. Thomas of Canterbury; a tune from Chaucer; catchy carols; and country dances.

At the foot of Capitol Hill, at the east end of the Mall, is the conservatory of the U.S. Botanic Garden. The Botanic Garden is funded by Congress and is open every day of the year. Since the late 1940's, the conservatory has been the site of a Christmas greens exhibition from Thanksgiving through New Year's Day. In recent years, a different theme has been chosen each year for the display. In 2002, the theme was "Holiday Sweets." Visitors strolled through a setting inspired by candy and other confections, touring the "lollipop forest" and admiring peppermint plants, chocolate trees, and other delights.

The majority of the buildings on the Mall are part of the Smithsonian Institution, which was founded when James Smithson, a British scientist, died in 1829. He left his entire estate—more than $500,000—to the United States with the instructions that an "establishment for the increase and diffusion of knowledge among men" be founded in his name. In the years since Smithson's bequest, the Smithsonian has become the world's largest museum complex. At Christmas, the Smithsonian's various individual facilities offer an extraordinary variety of programs.

COCCOLOBA
PUBESCENS

The holidays are celebrated at the Smithsonian's National Museum of American History with an annual festival of performing arts and crafts that features music, song, dance, and demonstrations of holiday traditions in foods and crafts from around the nation and the world. Each year the venue is different.

The Smithsonian Institution often offers workshops and classes on various subjects for all the holidays celebrated at this time of year, including Christmas, Hanukkah, Kwanzaa, and New Year's. Instructions in crafts in past years have included the making of gingerbread houses, evergreen wreaths, paper angels, and straw ornaments. A child-adult workshop has been offered in the Japanese art of origami, or paper folding. Participants learned to make a variety of holiday ornaments—for example, paper strawberries, stars, candy canes, and pandas.

Also in years past, the National Museum of American History has hosted holiday celebrations with jugglers, mimes, handbell ringers, barbershop quartets, Jewish instrumental music, Renaissance music and dance, movies, puppet shows, caroling, madrigal singers, and readings of holiday literature. Craftspeople throughout the museum have demonstrated their art: the making of teddy bears; the

In front of the black granite wall at the Vietnam Veterans Memorial* (insert), *visitors leave holiday cards in honor of deceased loved ones. At the United States Botanic Garden* (left), *poinsettias in bloom wear the colors of the season.

The Capitol Christmas tree lights up the D.C., night sky. The national forest from which the tree is taken is chosen five years in advance.

carving of wooden nutcrackers; the baking of Jewish holiday cookies; the making of menorahs—the Jewish ceremonial candelabras; the fashioning of all kinds of holiday stars—Danish paper stars, Moravian Herrnhut stars, Polish stars, and even Filipino star lanterns. Utilizing its collection of antique presses, the museum somtimes offers demonstrations of early printing techniques; at the end of the demonstration, audiences might be presented with a calendar, that they have watched being printed.

The Smithsonian Institution sponsors a variety of tours during December. Some are trips to distant places, such as the Christmas tours in Prague, London and Canterbury, and Quebec City; the "Christmas Markets on the Danube" cruise; and the Kenya Family Christmas Safari. But some are right in the Smithsonian's own backyard, so to speak. These have included the "Jewels of the Night" tour, an evening tour of famous D.C. landmarks, and the "Dining in the Nation's Capital" tour, in which participants enjoy meals in some of the city's finest restaurants, which are decorated in their holiday finest.

Another branch of the Smithsonian Institution is the Anacostia Museum/Center for African-American History, which was founded in 1967 as a neighborhood museum serving African Americans in the Anacostia community. Today it is a national resource devoted to the identification, documentation, protection, and interpretation of the African American experience, focusing on

At the Heurich House Museum, evergreens and red ribbons festoon a chandelier and fireplace (left), *and an array of sumptuous sweets grace a sideboard* (right). *The structure was build in 1894 as the home of brewer Christian Heurich. It is a rare surviving example of a turn-of-the-century Washington home in which a large percentage of original furnishings are intact.*

Washington, D.C. and the Upper South. Each year the museum hosts an annual Kwanzaa celebration with special workshops, ceremonies, and exhibits.

Kwanzaa is an African American holiday based on the traditional African festival of the harvest of the first crops. It begins on December 26 and lasts for seven days. But at the Anacostia Museum, the celebration begins early in December and lasts all month. On the first Saturday of the month, for example, the museum holds a Kwanzaa ceremony for the entire family. Other events include the Black Doll Show, the Black Gift Show, and the African-American Holiday Expo.

Throughout the year, the National Museum of Natural History, next door to its American History counterpart, draws crowds of children with its permanent exhibits of reconstructed dinosaurs and animal dioramas. During the Christmas season, the museum offers a variety of holiday programs and workshops for its young patrons.

Across the street from the National Museum of Natural History is the National Archives building. The National Archives preserves and makes available for research federal government records of enduring value. It also administers 11 presidential libraries at sites across the country. These presidential libraries contain a wide variety of materials related to Christmas. The Truman Library has president Harry S. Truman's 1951 Christmas gift list (the list of gifts the president received during that year of his presidency), which includes items such as "1 case tuna fish (48 7-oz. cans)," "beautiful bottle cognac," and a mystery item described only as "small gadget." The Herbert Hoover Presidential Library has an extensive online archive of material related to Christmas, including explanations of legends such as the Christmas pickle, candy canes, and snowmen. It also features a detailed record of past Christmas celebrations at the White House. And the Reagan Library and Museum has archived Ronald Reagan's Christmas Day radio addresses to the nation.

On the north side of the Mall, between 3rd and 7th Streets is the world, including the only painting by Leonardo da Vinci outside Europe.

During the year, the Gallery offers free "Gallery Talks," in which participants take guided tours of specific pieces of artwork in the Gallery. At Christmastime, these talks take on a special holiday theme. Offered at different times throughout the month of December is "The Christmas Story in Art," in which a Gallery lecturer leads a tour of works in the collection related to Christmas.

And for those who enjoy the outdoors, the National Gallery of Art is home to a sculpture garden, in the six-acre block adjacent to the west building. Since the late

Christmas at the National Gallery is not a matter of decoration; here, the holiday is celebrated with art.

august National Gallery of Art. At Christmas, banks of red poinsettias circle the Mercury-crowned, marble fountain in the center of the Rotunda. But Christmas at the National Gallery is not a matter of decoration; here, the holiday is celebrated with art.

The National Gallery, which is affiliated with the Smithsonian but governed by its own board of trustees, houses one of the finest collections of Western art in the

1960's, the reflecting pool and fountain in the garden have been transformed into a public ice-skating rink during the winter months. The sculpture garden was renovated in 1999 and is even more spectacular now.

Christmas on the nation's "main street," like Christmas on Main Streets everywhere, includes holiday shopping. Both Washingtonians and tourists have found that the Mall is a good place to find unique gifts of su-

A bronze lion, cast from an original at St. Peter's in Rome, is dressed for Christmas at Washington's Corcoran Gallery of Art.

perb quality. Most of the museums' gift shops offer holiday items unlike those available at department stores and shopping centers.

Although the National Mall is brimming with Christmas shoppers and sightseers, its enormous length and breadth offer both breathing space in the center of a hectic city and places of quiet contemplation. Along the drives, the rows of graceful, winter-bare trees frosted with ice and snow or even shrouded in Potomac fog, provide a scene of ethereal beauty. These trees, one of the nation's largest stands of the disease-prone American elm, are themselves something of a living museum, a beautiful but sad reminder of what the streets of most American cities and towns have lost.

Under these trees, people stroll, summer and winter, past the Tidal Basin and the Jefferson Memorial, toward the templelike Lincoln Memorial, and beyond, north, to a more recent shrine—the black granite Vietnam Veterans Memorial. Although this is one of the most visited sites in Washington, it is a quiet place. Here, every day, including Christmas, silent pilgrims come to remember loved ones lost in that agonizing war. Wreaths are left along the wall, and cards are taped under the names of sons and daughters, spouses, and friends. The sight of those cards propped along the black, mirror-like wall is a powerful image, a potent reminder of the meaning of the words *peace on earth*.

The Washington, or National, Cathedral is constructed entirely of handcut stone and sits on Mount St. Alban—the site George Washington selected for a national house of prayer.

The word Advent *comes from the Latin word* adventus, *which means a coming or arrival.*

In suburban Kensington, Maryland, the grounds of the Mormon Temple are decorated for Christmas with thousands of miniature lights.

In Christian churches, the term Advent signifies the coming of the Christ child and is celebrated through the four weeks before Christmas. The Advent season, thus begins on the Sunday nearest St. Andrew's Day, which is November 30, and continues until midnight, December 24, which marks the beginning of the Christmas season. In many churches, the Christmas season then continues until Epiphany, January 6, which in Western Christian churches is the day on which the coming of the Wise Men to the Christ child is celebrated.

In Washington, D.C., Advent and the twelve days of Christmas are celebrated in ways familiar to all Americans of the Christian faith. But as the nation's capital, Washington is a unique place. Institutions in the capital tend to be national, rather than local, in scope and intent. The churches of Washington are no exception. Most of the world's religions are represented in the city; Washington contains nearly 300 churches of 60 different faiths. They tend to be larger in scale than a city the size of Washington might warrant, and they tend to display a national, rather than local, outlook. Unofficially, the nation's capital has become a world religious center.

Many Washington churches that are not identified as national institutions are locally associated with great historic traditions: the New York Avenue Presbyterian Church is known as "Lincoln's Church." The church's Civil War era pastor, Reverend Phineas D. Gurley, conducted Lincoln's funeral services here. The present church, rebuilt in 1948, contains the original Lincoln pew.

St. John's Episcopal Church on Lafayette Square is known as the "Church of Presidents." In 1816, a committee was formed to "wait on the President of the United States (James Madison) and offer him a pew in this church, without his being obliged to purchase same." Madison chose a pew, but he payed the annual rental. Presidents Monroe, Adams, Jackson, Van Buren, and Harrison occupied the same pew. It has since been set aside for presidents. In fact, every president has occupied the pew at least once.

St. Matthew's Roman Catholic Cathedral, on Rhode Island Avenue, is associated with President Kennedy, who often attended Mass there. It was in St. Matthew's that funeral services were held for him.

This combination of national interest and local history produces great traditions. These traditions are very apparent in the city's many Advent and Christmas worship services, which display great variety as well as signs of painstaking preparation. Of the many ecclesiastical services scheduled in Washington during Advent and the twelve days of Christmas, three programs stand out as being of national prominence: the Christmas Eve Mass at the Basilica of the National Shrine of the Immaculate Conception; the Advent and Christmas services at the Cathedral of SS. Peter and Paul, or the National Cathedral; and the Christmas Eve service at the Franciscan Monastery, which is affiliated with Washington's Catholic University of America.

The Basilica of the National Shrine of the Immaculate Conception, on the campus of the Catholic University of America, was designed to be "the greatest church edifice in the Western Hemisphere." It is the largest Catholic church in America. Generations of American Roman Catholics, as well as three popes, contributed to the building, which was begun in 1920.

Dating back to ancient Greek and Roman times, a basilica originally was a type of public building in which official business was conducted. Beginning in the 300's, basilicas began to be used as places of worship. It was during this time that the construction of the great basilicas of Rome was begun. Soon these basilica churches began to play a unique role in the life of the Popes in the universal church.

Today the term *basilica* refers to a special designation given by the Pope to certain churches because of their antiquity, dignity, historical importance, or significance as a center of worship and devotion. The National Shrine was named a basilica on October 12, 1990 by Pope John Paul II.

The Basilica of the National Shrine is the largest Catholic church in the Western Hemisphere and the eighth largest in the world. It measures a total of 459 feet long and covers an area of 77,500 square feet. Each year, more than half a million people journey to this sacred shrine for worship.

At the Basilica of the National Shrine, Advent culminates on Christmas Eve. In the late afternoon the Shrine celebrates a Children's Christmas Mass and Gospel Pageant in the Great Upper Church.

Then at 9 p.m., the Christmas Eve service begins with a series of musical celebrations. Roman Catholics from around the city and the nation arrive early on Christmas Eve to be assured a seat. The music continues through the evening until finally the Solemn Eucharist is celebrated at 10:30 p.m.

On Christmas Day, the Basilica of the National Shrine celebrates Masses throughout the day. At noon, a Solemn Eucharist is celebrated by the Archbishop of Washington. At 5:00 p.m., a children's Mass is celebrated, with a children's choir and a group of young people reenacting the story of Christ's birth. And in an effort to reach out to those who are alone and in need on Christmas Day, the Basilica of the National Shrine hosts a Christmas Dinner in the Shrine's dining room.

The seat of the Protestant Episcopal Diocese of Washington—SS. Peter and Paul—is known as the Washington, or National, Cathedral. Unlike parish churches, the Cathedral has no regular membership. Its doors are open to everyone. While the Cathedral's own services conducted by the clergy of the Cathedral are Episcopal, special services are often held by various denominations, each according to its own traditions. Religious leaders of many different affiliations preach from the Cathedral's pulpit.

The National Cathedral is not supported by the Washington Diocese or by the Episcopal Church. It is maintained by offerings and gifts from people of many different church affiliations. The Cathedral, by charter with the Congress of the United States, is

A Christmas tree, poinsettias, and swags of evergreens decorate a Nativity scene* (insert) *at the National Shrine of the Immaculate Conception, the largest Roman Catholic church in the Western Hemisphere. Christmas services at the Shrine* (right) *include a Christmas Eve midnight Mass.

Christmas Eve Holy Communion before the altar at St. John's Church, the "Church of Presidents."

legally obligated to function as a "House of Prayer for All People."

Construction of the National Cathedral, which was begun in 1907, was completed in 1990. Gothic in style, it is medieval in construction; that is, the Cathedral was built exactly as Gothic cathedrals were built in the 1300's—entirely of stone worked by hand. While the nave is 100 feet from floor to ceiling vault, no steel was used in the building of walls or roofs. Exterior flying buttresses support the great height of the walls of the nave. Both the interior and exterior are richly carved with figures that symbolize passages from the Old and New Testaments. Magnificent stained-glass windows illustrate more Biblical stories: rose windows represent the *Seven Days of Creation*, the *Last Judgment*, and the *Church Triumphant*.

The story of the birth of Jesus Christ is told in stone and stained glass in the Cathedral's Bethlehem Chapel. The foundation stone of the Cathedral, which lies directly under the altar of the Bethlehem Chapel, was brought from the Shepherds' Field outside Bethlehem. The five stained-glass windows of the ambulatory (the passage around the chapel altar) depict the genealogy of Christ, the appearance of the angels to the shepherds, the Annunciation, the Epiphany, and Simeon's acknowledgment of the Holy Child as the Christ.

Advent begins at the National Cathedral with Lessons and Carols on the first Sunday of Advent. On an evening in December, the Cathedral hosts an open house, in which its doors are opened to the public. Visitors are treated to music, refreshments, Christmas crafts demonstrations, and an opportunity to catch a spectacular view of Washington by night from the Pilgrim Observation Gallery. To the delight of youngsters, a number of children's activities are planned for this night—including a visit from Old St. Nick. And for those looking for just the right gift, the Cathedral's shops offer unique items and are open late this night.

In preparation for Holy Communion on Christmas Eve, the Cathedral's Altar Guild decorates the high altar, which is constructed of 12 stones from Solomon's quarry in Jerusalem. Many pounds of boxwood, Douglas fir, holly, as well as magnolia are used to decorate throughout the Cathedral. Lighted evergreen trees and wreaths twinkle from the shadows of the many chapels.

The magnificent architecture, the superb craftsmanship shown in the construction, the lavish and handsome decorations, and the very real ecumenical spirit make Holy Communion on Christmas Eve in the National Cathedral a memorable experience. Cathedral worship services continue on Christmas Day; normally one is nationally televised. The Cathedral remains decorated through Epiphany, January 6. The public is, of course, welcome to attend services and programs or to simply tour the buildings and gardens. However, because the Christmas Eve Eucharist is so popular, participants must obtain free tickets in advance by writing to the Cathedral earlier in the year.

During some Christmas seasons, the Cathedral gardens are the center of a great deal of attention. Here stands a thorn tree planted in 1900 by the first Episcopal bishop of Washington, Henry Yates Satterlee. While visiting England, Bishop Satterlee was given a slip from the famous Glastonbury Thorn. By tradition, the Glastonbury Thorn sprang from Joseph of Arimathea's staff, which was said to have been cut from the same tree that supplied the crown of thorns. (Joseph of Arimathea, who offered his tomb for the burial of Christ, is believed to have introduced Christianity into Britain.) The original thorn tree was destroyed by Oliver Cromwell's soldiers during the English civil war, but cuttings of it had already been planted elsewhere. Legend aside, the Glastonbury Thorn blooms both summer and winter. The second bloom usually comes at Christmas—in honor, it is said, of the birth of Jesus.

Bishop Satterlee's slip, which he planted on the grounds of the new cathedral being constructed in Washington, first bloomed on Christmas in 1918. In 1997, the tree planted here began to rot. It had to be replaced with a cutting from the original slip, which is maintained by the U.S. Botanic Gardens.

On Christmas Eve, Christians of all denominations gather at Washington's Fransican Monastery Memorial Church of the Holy Land. Here are facsimiles of the Chief Shrines of the Christian religion: the Garden of Gethsemane, the Holy Sepulchre, the Catacombs of Rome, and the Grotto of Bethlehem. The Franciscan Monastery's Grotto of Bethlehem is a faithful reproduction of the Grotto of the Nativity in Bethlehem. At exactly the hour at which the Christmas Eve service is held in Bethlehem an identical service is held in Washington. When the Christmas Eve Mass is completed, a procession headed by a cross bearer winds its way through the Monastery Church. With great care, one of the celebrants carries a life-sized wooden image of the Infant. Descending a spiral staircase, the procession reaches the crypt. The altar stands between two flights of stairs. Below the altar is a facsimile of the silver star that in Bethlehem marks the spot where Jesus is believed to have been born. Upon arriving in the grotto the deacon chants the gospel of the first Mass of Christmas. With the words "and she brought forth her first-born son," the wooden image of the Infant is placed upon the star, which bears the inscription, in Latin, "Here Jesus Christ was born of the Virgin Mary." When the deacon reads "and wrapped him in swaddling clothes," the image is raised from the star and carried to the Place of the Manger, which is two steps below and to the right of the star. The ceremony concludes when the image of the Baby Jesus is layed into the straw arranged in the manger. The long procession of celebrants climbs up the stairs, winds its way through the church, and out into the night. It is Christmas morning. The Christ is born.

A National Cathedral Christmas service for children includes a living Nativity scene in the Bethlehem Chapel. Below this chapel is the Cathedral cornerstone, which is made of stones collected from the Shepherds' Field outside of Bethlehem.

Home for Christmas

Although Washington has its share of government officials who flee the town at Christmastime, the city is not as transient as many believe it to be. Washington families gather together at this season to attend church, to share Christmas dinner, to exchange gifts, to enjoy the beauty of the often snow-clad city, and to reminisce about former Christmases in this historic town.

Few have been around long enough to recall the very old sights and sounds of Christmases past, but they have heard stories of Christmas in old Washington. One hundred years ago, most

Today, fashionable Washingtonians Christmas shop in such lavishly decorated malls as Georgetown Park **(left)*****. Long ago, the fashionable, including presidents and first ladies, shopped late—Christmas Eve—along Pennsylvania Avenue.***

EXIT

Washington's venerable Willard Hotel is decorated for the holidays exactly as it was in its heyday as the city's center of political intrigue. Lincoln was smuggled into the Willard before his inauguration; Julia Ward Howe wrote "The Battle Hymn of the Republic" during a stay at the hotel.

families made a trip to the Centre Market on 7th Street and Pennsylvania Avenue, where the National Archives now stands, to purchase a Christmas tree and greenery. During Christmas week, farmers came to the market with wagons full of evergreen, holly, mistletoe, and laurel. At that time, every church and home was draped with greens for the holidays. Some said greenery was more plentiful than meat and vegetables. But the stalls inside the market also sold the food necessary for an ample Christmas dinner—vegetables, hams and turkeys, fruits and nuts. Today, the Eastern Market near Capitol Hill stands as the last example of this old Washington tradition.

Washingtonians, like most Americans, do their Christmas shopping in multileveled shopping malls, such as Georgetown Park with its Victorian arcade shops, green wrought iron and shining brass trim, and skylit atrium. Georgetown Park is always lavishly decorated for Christmas and provides costumed musicians and carolers to entertain shoppers. Although some Washingtonians remain loyal to the one remaining, stately downtown department store, the days of bustling open-air Christmas shopping, where once even the nation's president could be seen selecting Christmas gifts, are nearly over.

The dome of the Capitol is visible in the night sky beyond the massive Union Station entry arch with its illuminated wreath.

President Abraham Lincoln often visited a toy shop that stood near 12th Street and New York Avenue. There he bought toy soldiers for his sons. President Taft enjoyed shopping on Pennsylvania Avenue. He would go on foot accompanied by an aide, and both would return long after dark laden with bundles. President Warren G. Harding often made Christmas purchases for friends in a Washington bookstore. Not wanting to be noticed, he went late, walked briskly, wore a dark coat, and pulled his hat down low.

For good or for bad, many old Washington Christmas traditions have disappeared forever: the firecrackers, pistol shots, and general rowdiness of Christmas Eve celebrations; the wartime Christmases, when Washington families took servicemen into their homes for dinner; and the sight of Santa, his pack on his back, arriving at the Navy Yard on Christmas morning to distribute packages to each house in the long row of quarters, as the sound of the Navy Band playing carols drifted up and down the street.

But Washington remembers, in its own way, Yuletides of long ago. The long-time residents of

A Washington, D.C. family gathers to open gifts on Christmas morning.

the city still keep old traditions. Some take a Christmas candlelight tour of Old Town Alexandria, George Washington's hometown, and enjoy music and refreshments in historic homes. Others spend time during the holidays at Washington's Rock Creek Park, where they join the miller and hear folk tales told around the old pot-belly stove. Others delight in the history of the

Georgetown's homes and businesses alike wear their Christmas finery.

Santa talks to a girl at the Georgetown Park shopping center in Washington, D.C.

Willard Hotel, the center of Washington politics in the mid-1800's, now a restored landmark, which is beautifully decorated for the holidays.

As the season comes to a close, the citizens of Washington prepare for the last of the holiday celebrations—the ringing in of the new year.

The Kennedy Center for the Performing Arts is the scene of merriment for Washingtonians, who ring in the New Year in the Grand Foyer to the strains of "Auld Lang Syne."

At the Kennedy Center, Washingtonians, dressed in ball gowns and tuxedos, waltz through New Year's Eve in the Center's Grand Foyer. However they choose to observe the New Year, the people of Washington celebrate the end of one year and the beginning of another. Another year to add to history in a city where the making of history never stops.

Crafts

Stencil Patterns

Material list:
- tracing paper
- construction paper
- tissue paper
- pencil
- snub-nosed scissors
- poster paint
- 1-square-inch piece of sponge

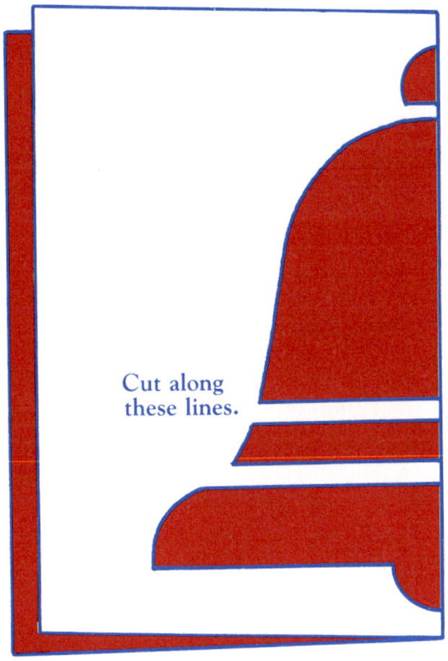

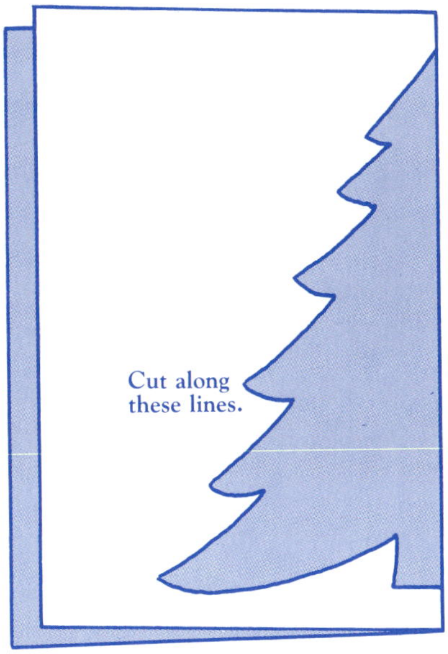

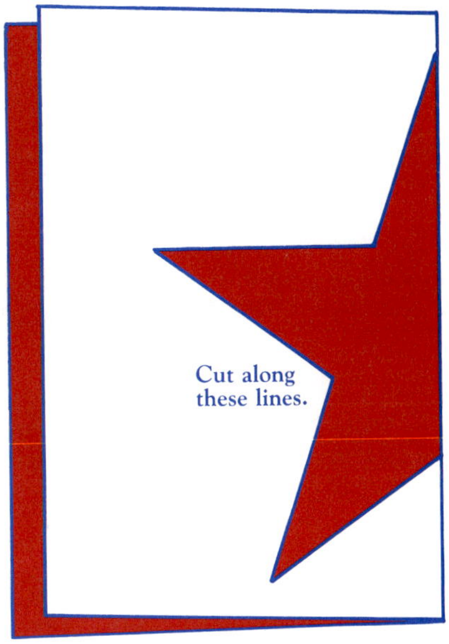

To make the bell, tree, and star stencils:

(1) Trace patterns on tracing paper and cut them out.

(2) Cut construction paper into 4-inch by 3-inch pieces, and fold into 2-inch by 3-inch pieces.

(3) Place one of the patterns on a piece of folded construction paper, lining up the right side of the pattern with the fold in the paper. Outline the pattern onto the construction paper.

(4) Cut along the lines you traced and unfold the paper. You now have a stencil.

Point A

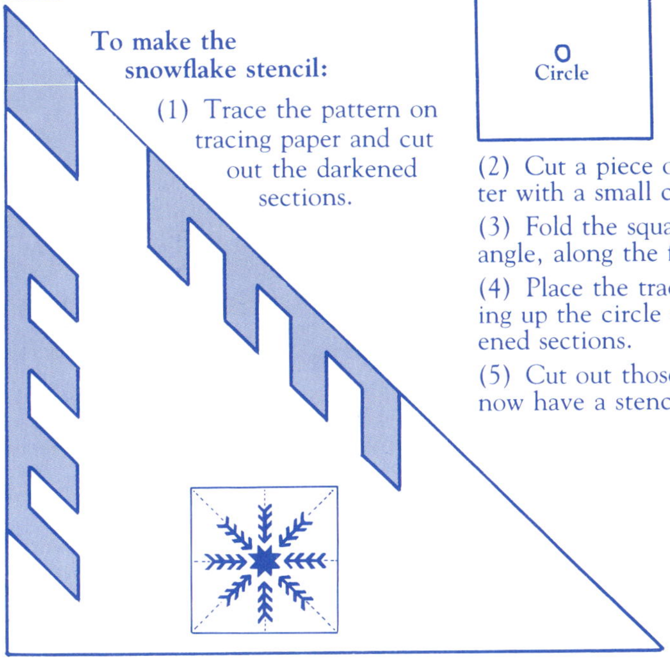

To make the snowflake stencil:

(1) Trace the pattern on tracing paper and cut out the darkened sections.

(2) Cut a piece of construction paper 5 inches square. Mark its center with a small circle. As you fold the square, keep the circle visible.

(3) Fold the square in half, then in half again, and then into a triangle, along the fold line extending from the circle.

(4) Place the tracing paper over the folded construction paper, lining up the circle with point A on the pattern, and trace the darkened sections.

(5) Cut out those sections and unfold the construction paper. You now have a stencil, as pictured in the inset to the left.

To make Christmas wrapping paper:

(1) Lightly tape stencil to tissue paper.

(2) Dip sponge into water-thinned poster paint and pat open area of stencil.

(3) Repeat with same or different stencil to complete wrapping paper.

Uncle Sam Ornament

Material list:
- cardboard tube from toilet paper roll
- bond paper
- crayons or markers
- pencil
- tape
- glue (preferably a stick glue)
- string or yarn
- snub-nosed scissors

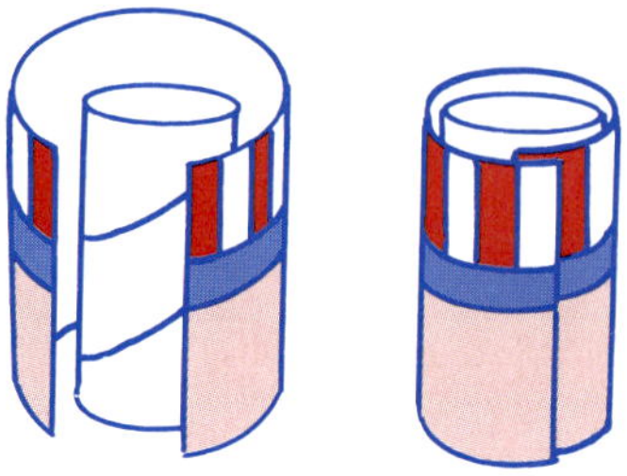

(1) Trace pattern A on bond paper, and color with markers or crayons as shown in the pattern.

(2) Trim the excess bond paper and glue the pattern onto the cardboard tube, the white and red stripes being parallel to the length of the tube.

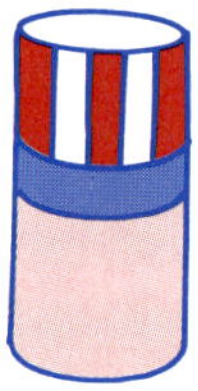

(3) Trace pattern B on bond paper, and color one side blue. Cut out the pattern. If the marker has bled through, trace another pattern B, cut it out, and glue it to the white side of the first pattern.

(4) Using the pencil, poke a hole through the black dot in the center of the hat brim. Then, cut carefully along the lines, radiating from the center.

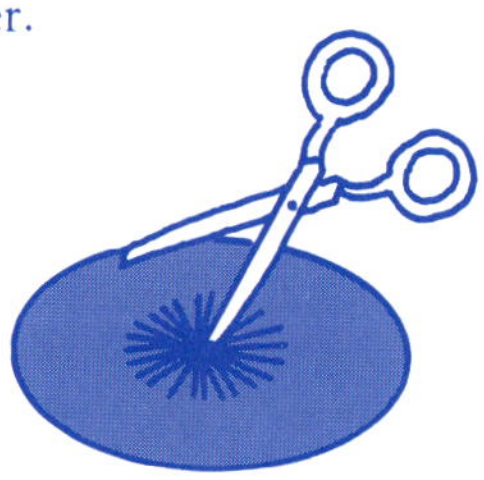

Pattern A

(5) Place the cardboard tube on the table, pink side up. Spread a little glue around the pink part of the tube, just above the blue stripe. Holding the hat brim (white side up) over the tube, push the tube up through the center of the hat brim until the blue stripe on the tube meets the hat brim.

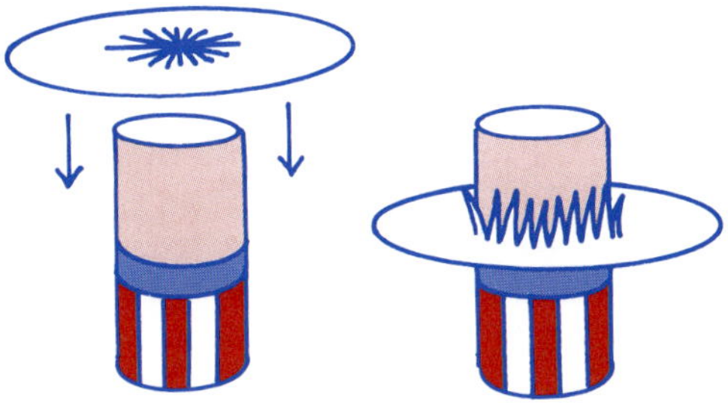

(6) Trace pattern C on bond paper, and cut it out, also carefully cutting along the parallel lines. Glue the beard one-half inch from the bottom of the pink area.

(7) Trace patterns D, E, and F. Color the nose pink, the berry red, and the leaf green. Cut them out. Place glue only on the top of the nose and attach it halfway between the white beard and the hat brim. Glue the berry to the leaf and attach to the hat as shown in the illustration.

(8) With a black marker, draw in the eyes and mouth as shown in the illustration.

(9) Poke a hole near the top of the hat for the yarn or string. Tie and hang up.

Pattern B

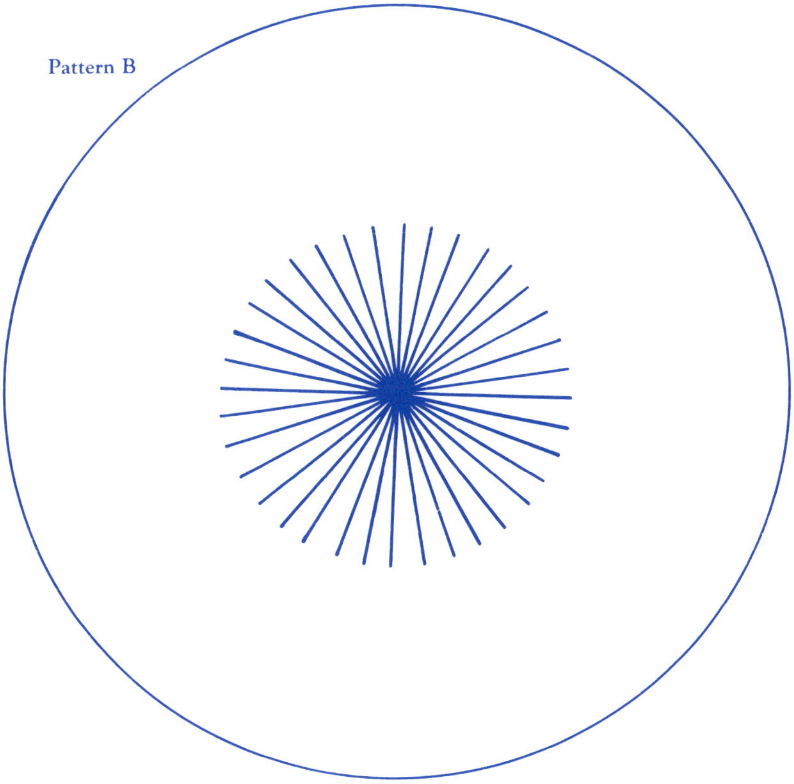

Pattern D

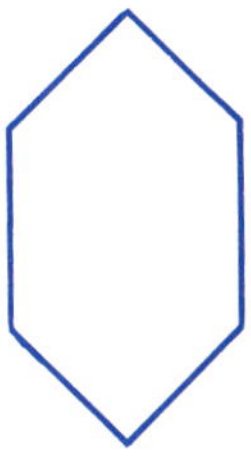

Pattern E

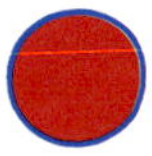

Pattern F

Pattern C

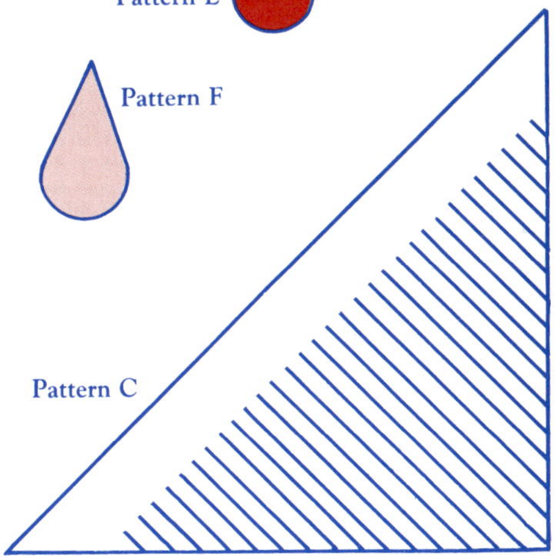

Christmas Star Mobile

Material list:
- pencil
- cardboard
- tracing paper
- snub-nosed scissors
- straight pins
- white and green yarn
- tape
- hair spray or spray starch
- thread
- drinking straws, cut into three 3-inch lengths
- heavy cardboard

(1) Cut tracing paper and cardboard into 3-inch squares.

(2) Trace the star and Christmas tree patterns (figures 1 & 2) onto the tracing paper and tape each to a square of cardboard. Insert pins, as in figures 3 & 4.

(3) Cut an 18-inch piece of white yarn for the star, green for the tree.

(4) Wrap the yarn in and out of the pins as in figures 3 & 4. Tape the ends to the edge of the cardboard.

(5) Spray the yarn until soaked with hair spray or spray starch. Let dry completely.

Figure 1

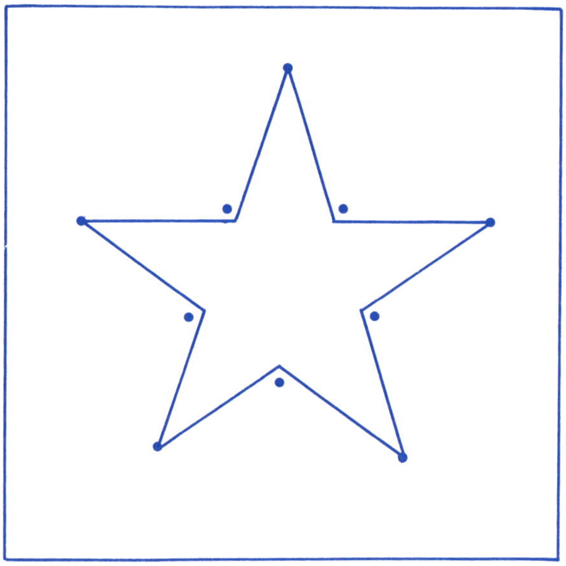

Figure 3

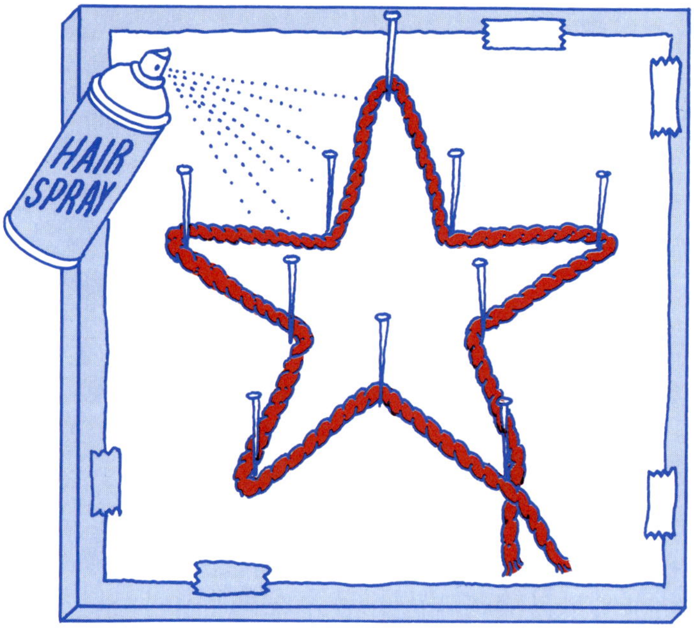

Figure 2

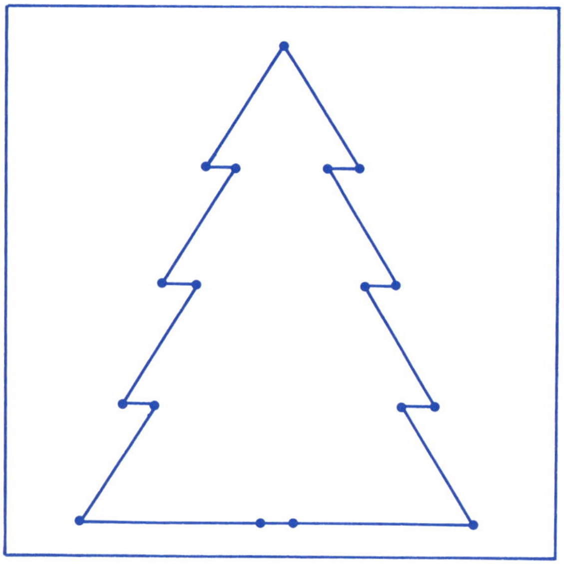

Figure 4

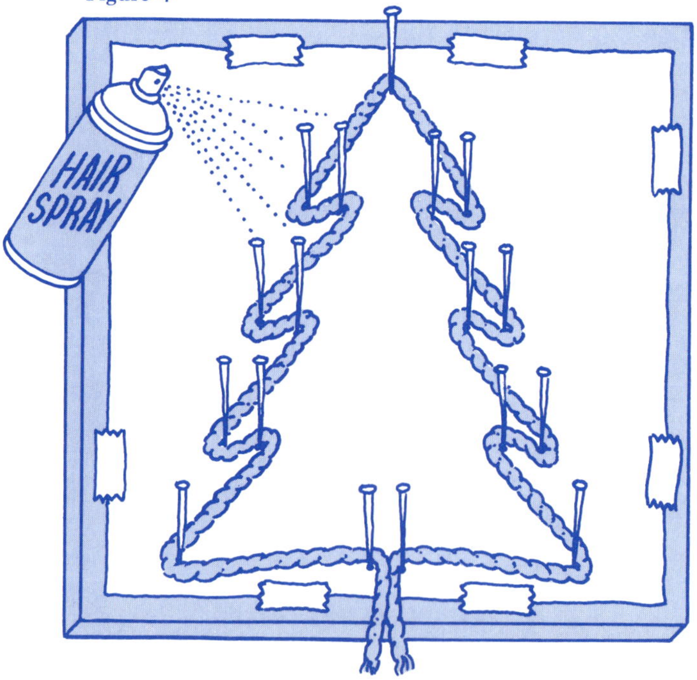

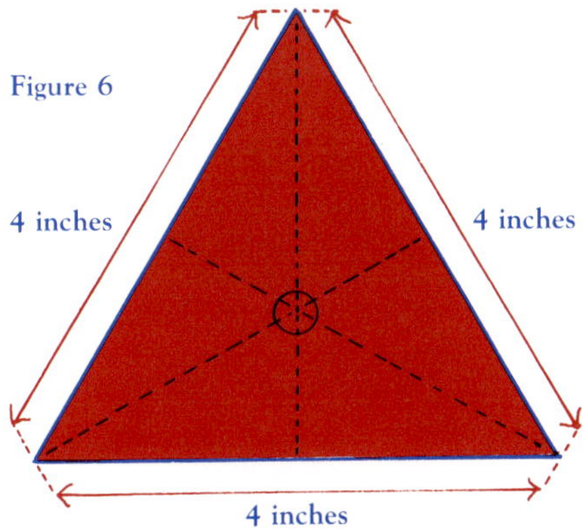

Figure 6

(10) Cut a triangle, 4 inches on each side, out of the heavy cardboard, as in figure 6. Make a hole at each of the corners and in the center. Attach a string to the center.

(11) Tie a different length of string to the center of each straw. Tie the other end of the string to one of the triangle's corners. You can now hang up your mobile.

(6) Untape and remove the star and tree. Trim the ends of the yarn.

(7) Make 2 more stars and 2 more trees.

(8) Tie different lengths of string to the tops of each ornament.

(9) Attach an ornament to each end of the 3 straws, as in figure 5.

Figure 5

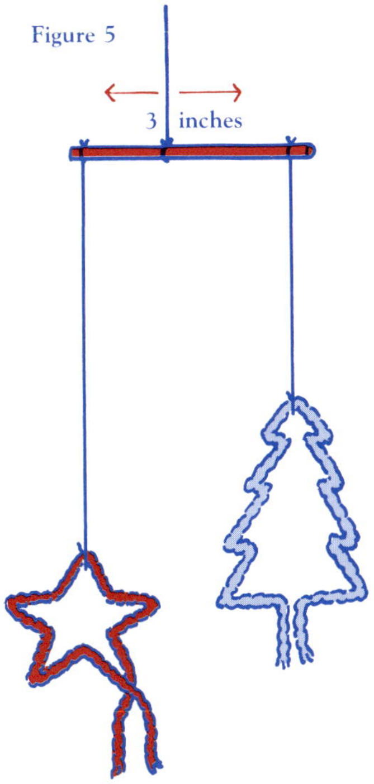

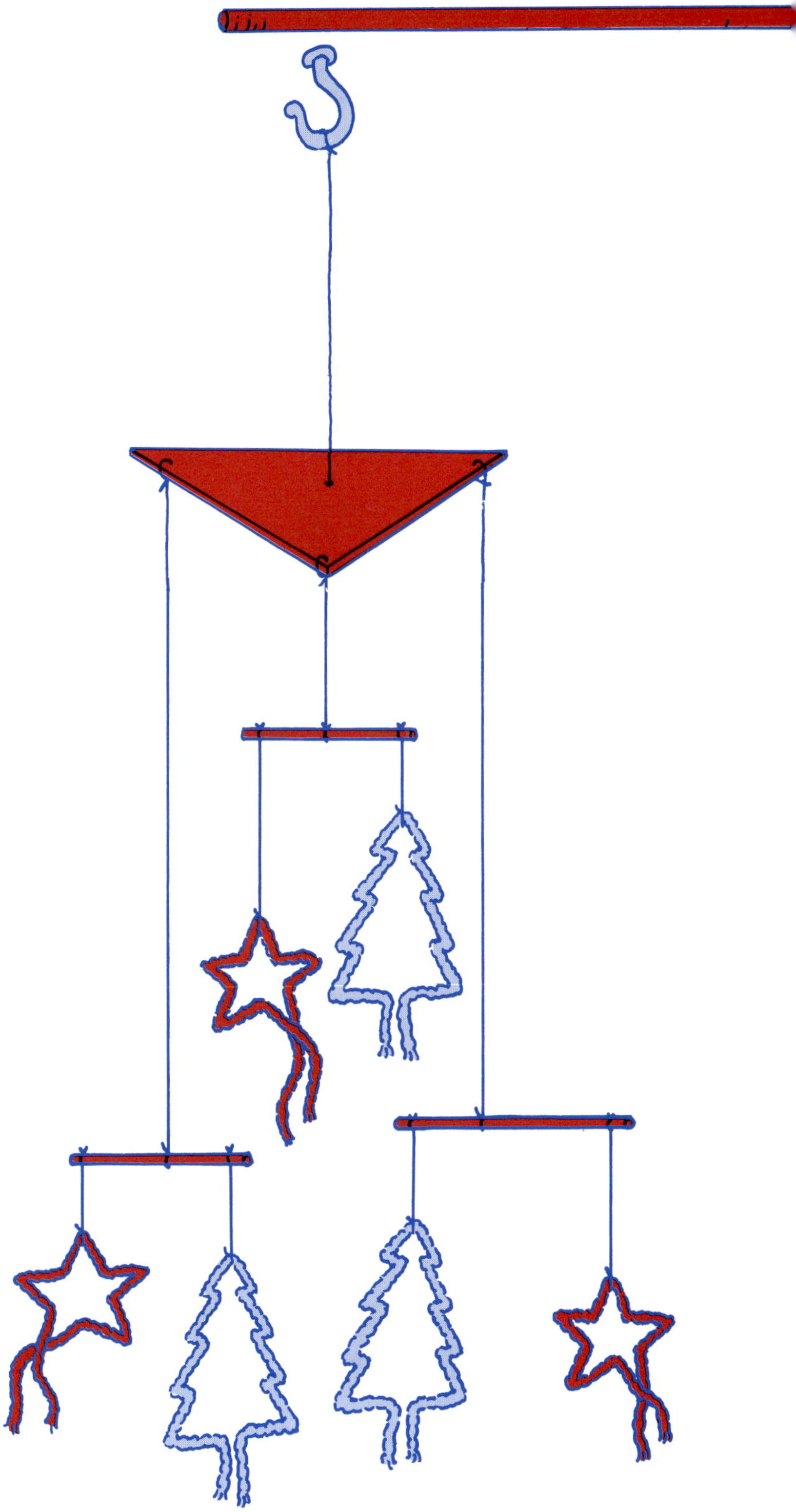

Garland Paper Chain

Material list:
- red paper, white paper, blue paper
- glue
- pencil
- snub-nosed scissors
- tape

(1) Cut the paper into strips ½″ by 5½″.

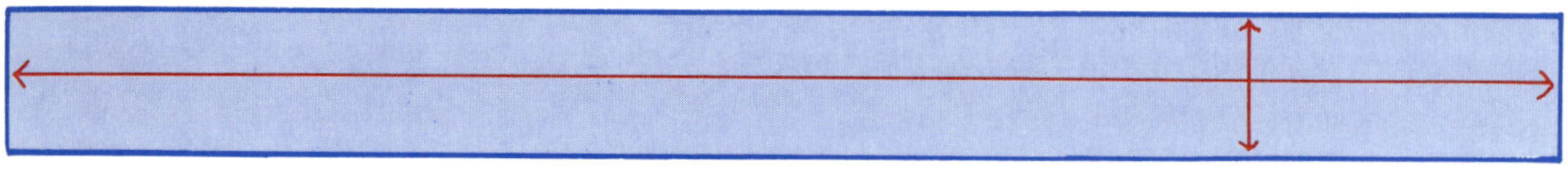

(2) Take both ends of a paper strip and join them together with glue.

(3) Take another strip of paper; put it through the first ring; and join both ends together with glue.

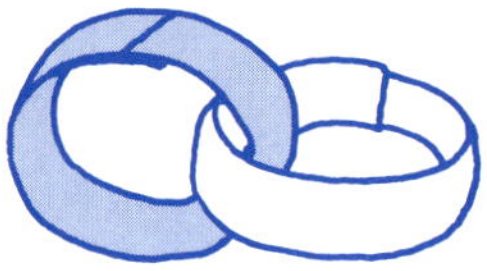

(4) The rings can be strung together in repetition of a regular color pattern, in random color patterns, or in a garland all of one color. Continue adding strips of paper until you have reached the length you desire.

(5) Different lengths of garland can be taped to a door or wall in the form of a Christmas tree. Cut out the tree base from blue paper, and the star from white paper, using the patterns and dimensions below. Use red paper for the candles, and yellow for the flames, following the pattern and dimensions below. Arrange the pieces as in the illustration below, and tape to the door or wall.

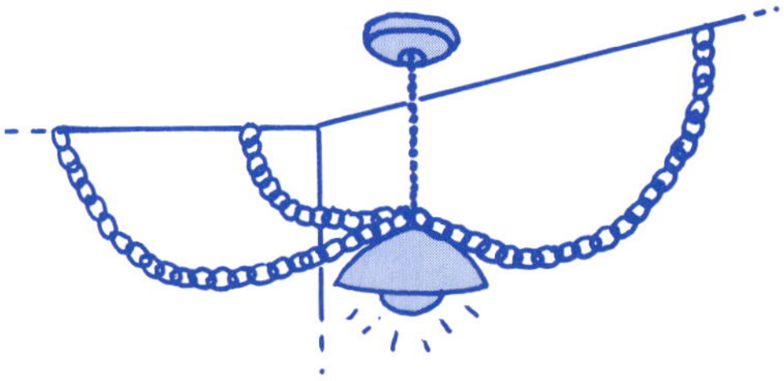

(6) Garlands can also be suspended from a chandelier to the edges of the ceiling.

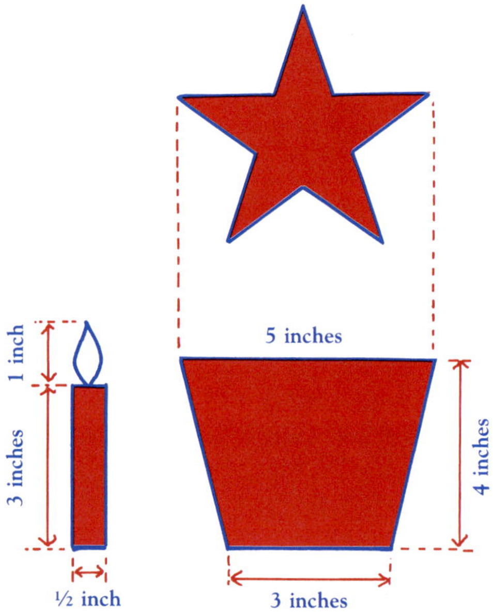

(7) Long garlands can be used to decorate a Christmas tree.

Christmas Door Decoration

Material list:
- thick color paper
- snub-nosed scissors
- needle and thread
- tracing paper or thin bond paper
- tape
- pencil
- red or green ribbon bow

(1) Trace each of the patterns below onto separate pieces of tracing paper or thin bond paper. Cut them out.

(2) Cut out 2 pieces of the thick color paper, 3″ by 4″. Fold them in half along the 4″ length. Tape each pattern onto a piece of the folded paper, lining up the right edge of the pattern with the fold in the color paper.

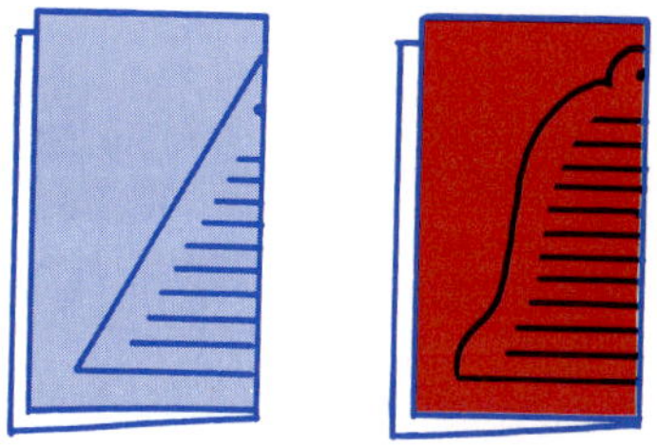

(3) Cut along each of the solid, parallel lines; then along the outlines of the tree and bell. Open them out flat.

(4) On a piece of the color paper, draw a stem and a clapper, each about 3″ long. Follow the shapes pictured here. Cut them out.

(5) Weave the stem up the center of the tree, in and out of the slits. Do the same with the clapper. Then twist the stem and clapper 90 degrees, so that the tree and bell "open up." Using the needle, loop a piece of thread through their tops.

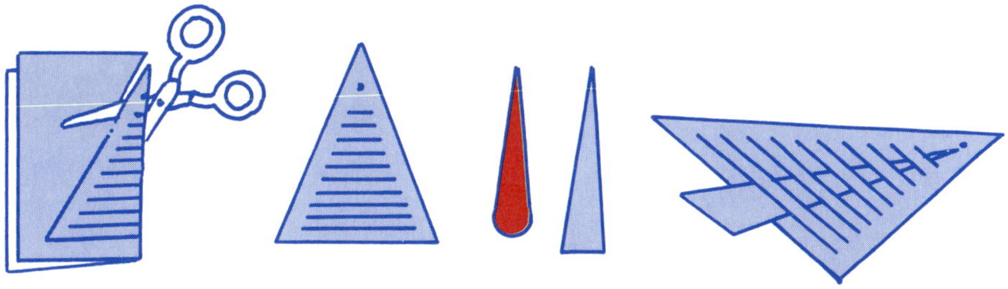

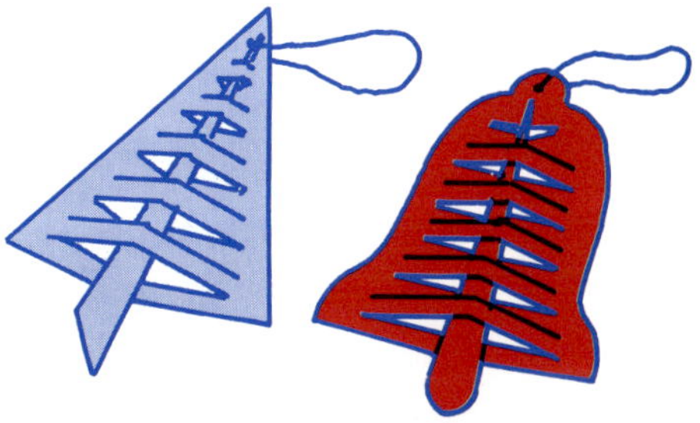

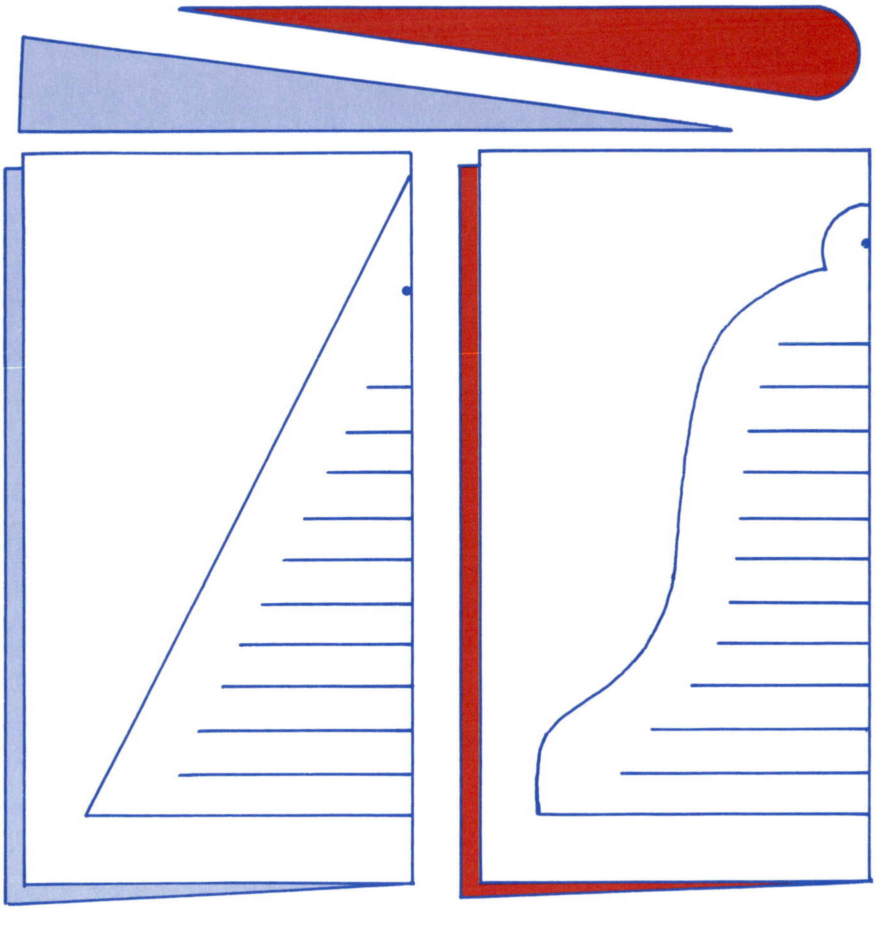

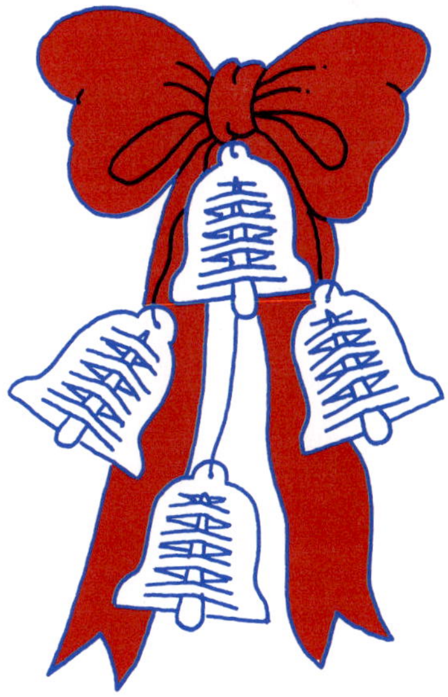

(6) Make as many ornaments as you need for the ribbon bow. Then attach them to the bow, as shown above.

Recipes
from the White House

Mrs. Lyndon B. Johnson's POPOVERS

1 c. sifted all-purpose flour
¼ t. salt
2 eggs, beaten
1 c. milk
2 tbs. shortening, melted

Combine flour and salt in a bowl. Blend together last 3 ingredients. Gradually add these to the dry ingredients, beating constantly about 1 minute, or until batter is smooth. Fill greased sizzling-hot pans ¾ full and bake at 450° F. 20 minutes. Reduce heat to 350° F. and continue baking 15 to 20 minutes, or until deep golden brown.

8 medium popovers

Andrew Jackson's SPOON BREAD

1 c. white hominy grits or water-ground white corn meal
1½ t. salt
1 c. cold water
2 c. hot milk
2 eggs, beaten
3 tbs. butter or margarine

Stir together first 3 ingredients until smooth. Blend in hot milk. Cook and stir over low heat until mixture begins to thicken. Remove from heat. Blend in eggs and butter. Turn into a well-greased 1-quart casserole. Bake at 350° F. 45 minutes, or until firm to the touch. Serve with a spoon from the casserole with plenty of butter or margarine.

About 6 servings

Martha Washington's SPICED GYNGERBREDE

2¾ c. sifted all-purpose flour
1 t. baking soda
½ t. salt
2 t. ground ginger
1 t. ground cinnamon
1 t. ground mace
1 t. ground nutmeg
½ c. hydrogenated shortening
2 tbs. grated orange peel
½ c. packed brown sugar
3 eggs
¼ c. strained orange juice
¼ c. brandy
1 c. molasses

Sift the first 7 ingredients together and set aside. Thoroughly blend together the next 3 ingredients. Add eggs, one at a time, beating until light and fluffy after each addition. Mix heated orange juice and brandy with molasses. Alternately, add dry ingredients and molasses mixture to creamed mixture, beginning and ending with dry ingredients. After each addition, beat until blended. Turn batter into greased 9x9x2-inch baking pan. Bake at 350° F. 30 to 40 minutes. Let cool.

One 9-inch square gingerbread

ROAST LAMB WITH ELDERBERRY SAUCE

5-to 7-pound leg of lamb (boned)
3 c. crumbled corn bread
¼ c. minced parsley
½ t. salt
pinch of pepper
3 tbs. mint sauce
1 egg, beaten
¼ c. milk
elderberry sauce (see recipe below)

Toss together all the ingredients from corn bread to milk. Place this stuffing into the cavity left by deboning the leg of lamb. Fasten the opening and place lamb on a rack in a shallow roasting pan. Roast 35 minutes to the pound in a 300°–325°F. oven. When ready to serve, slice lamb and pour elderberry sauce over the slices.

6 to 8 servings

ELDERBERRY SAUCE

2 tbs. pan drippings
1½ tbs. flour
½ t. dry mustard
½ c. Burgundy
½ c. elderberry jelly
1 tbs. mixed grated orange and lemon peel

Stir dry mustard into a roux of pan drippings and flour. Gradually add wine, stirring constantly. Bring to boiling. Cook and stir 1 to 2 minutes. Add jelly and citrus peel. Heat and stir until jelly is melted and sauce is smooth.

About 1 cup sauce

Andrew Jackson's TURKEY HASH

medium-sized turkey (8 to 10 pounds)
celery
onion
1 bay leaf
salt
2 pods of red pepper
4 tbs. butter
2 tbs. flour
Worcestershire sauce
white pepper

Prepare turkey for a roaster. Add sufficient water to make stock. Put in next 5 ingredients. Cover; allow to cook slowly until tender. Do not brown. Pour off and strain stock; allow to cool. When fat rises to top, skim off and discard. When turkey has cooled, pull apart, discarding all skin, bones, and gristle. Cut in large, bite-sized pieces. Make a roux of the butter and flour in a large skillet or saucepan. Heat until bubbly. Stirring constantly, add gradually a quart of the turkey stock. Bring to boiling and cook 1 to 2 minutes. Season with Worcestershire sauce. To each quart of sauce, add 2 quarts of cut-up turkey. Add white pepper, if needed, and serve very hot.

8 to 10 servings

Teddy Roosevelt's CHRISTMAS TURKEY

18-pound turkey
1 dozen large oysters, minced very fine
2 c. fine bread crumbs
1 tbs. chopped herbs (parsley, thyme, or sweet marjoram)
salt
pepper

Prepare turkey for roasting. Combine the rest of the ingredients. Salt and pepper to taste. Stuff turkey and roast 4 to 4 ½ hours in a preheated 325°F. oven.

PHEASANTS WITH SPAETZLE

2 pheasants, cleaned and quartered
2 qt. boiling water
4 chicken bouillon cubes
½ c. flour
1 c. butter
1 t. paprika
7 tbs. flour
1 c. Chablis
1 c. dairy sour cream

Put necks, backs, giblets, etc. of pheasants and bouillon cubes into water. Cook until stock is reduced to 1½ quarts. Flour remaining pieces of pheasant. Saute in ½ cup butter until brown, and reserve. In large frying pan, melt ½ cup butter, add paprika and all but 1 cup of strained pheasant stock. Bring to boiling. Gradually stir in remaining stock and 7 tbs. flour. Boil 1 to 2 minutes. Stir in Chablis and cook gently 30 minutes. Add pheasant; cover and cook 1 to 1½ hours. Remove pheasant. Stir in sour cream, about a spoonful at a time, with gentle heating. Place pheasant in serving dish, spaetzle in a bowl. Over each, spoon some of the paprika sauce.

About 6 servings

SPAETZLE

3 eggs, beaten
½ t. salt
1 c. heavy cream
2 c. flour
chicken stock
¼ c. butter

Combine first 3 ingredients. Stir in flour to make a stiff batter. Dip a teaspoon into batter, just enough to cover the end of it. From end of teaspoon, drop batter into boiling chicken stock. Cook 5 minutes. Drain and saute in butter until light brown.

WILD RICE CASSEROLE

½ c. wild rice, soaked overnight
½ c. brown rice, soaked overnight
1 c. sliced fresh mushrooms
½ c. chopped white onion
½ c. shredded sharp cheddar cheese
6 tbs. cooking oil
1 c. hot chicken broth
2 tbs. sherry
salt and pepper
pimento strips

Drain rice, and combine with next 3 ingredients. Place in 1½-quart casserole or 8x8x2-inch baking dish. Stir in next 3 ingredients. Sprinkle with salt and pepper. Garnish with pimento strips. Bake at 350° F. 1 hour.

6 to 8 servings

Dolley Madison's FRYING HERBS

1½ pounds fresh spinach
½ c. chopped parsley
6 green onions
salt to taste
butter

Wash and drain spinach leaves and parsley. Chop parsley and onions. Combine all 3 ingredients in a pan with a bit of butter the size of a walnut and some salt. Cook over low heat, covered, until done. Serve with slices of broiled calf's liver, small rashers of bacon, and fried eggs—the latter on the herbs, the other in a separate dish.

About 4 servings

CUMIN-FLAVORED SPRING PEAS

½ t. cumin seed
¼ c. water
2 lb. fresh peas
¼ c. butter
6 green onions, chopped
½ c. heavy cream

Soak cumin seed in the water. Shell peas. One pound of peas unhulled is about 1 cup of young peas hulled. Saute onions in saucepan with butter until transparent, but not browned. Add cumin seed, water, and then peas. Add more water, if necessary. Cover and cook slowly until almost done, about 10–20 minutes. Add heavy cream; heat thoroughly; but do not boil.

4 servings

Martha Washington's FRUITED WHITE CAKE

1 c. butter
1 c. sugar
5 eggs, separated
2½ c. sifted all-purpose flour
1 t. ground mace
¼ t. ground nutmeg
1 c. diced assorted candied fruits
2 tbs. red wine
2 t. brandy

Cream butter. Beat in sugar gradually. Add egg yolks, one at a time, beating until fluffy after each addition. Sift spices with flour and combine with fruit. Combine everything and mix well. Blend in wine and brandy. Fold in egg whites, beaten until stiff, not dry, peaks are formed. Turn into greased (bottom only) and lightly floured 9-inch tube pan. Bake at 325° F. about 1¼ hours. Place pan on rack and let cool completely. Frosting may be used.

One 9-inch tubed fruit cake

Mrs. Harry Truman's OZARK PUDDING

1 egg
¾ c. sugar
¼ c. all-purpose flour
1¼ t. baking powder
⅛ t. salt
½ c. chopped nuts
½ c. chopped apple
1 t. vanilla extract

Beat together egg and sugar until thoroughly blended and smooth. Blend next 3 ingredients and mix into egg-sugar mixture. Stir in final ingredients. Turn into greased 8-inch pie pan. Bake at 350° F. about 35 minutes. Serve warm or cold with whipped cream or ice cream.

6 servings

Teddy Roosevelt's PHILADELPHIA SAND TARTS

1 c. butter
2 t. vanilla extract
2 c. sugar
2 eggs
1 egg, separated
4 c. sifted all-purpose flour
sugar and cinnamon

Cream butter and vanilla extract. Add sugar gradually, beating constantly until light and fluffy. Add eggs, one at a time, beating well after each addition. Beat in egg yolk, then blend in flour. Mix well. Chill, if necessary. Roll thin on lightly floured surface, cut with round cookie cutter 2½ inches in diameter. Brush with remaining egg white, slightly beaten. Sprinkle with sugar and cinnamon. Place on greased cookie sheets and bake at 350° F. 8 to 10 minutes.

About 6 dozen cookies

PLANTATION POUND CAKE

1 lb. butter
½ t. lemon extract
½ t. freshly grated nutmeg
10 eggs, separated
1 lb. confectioners' sugar, sifted
1 lb. all-purpose flour, sifted (4c.)
1 tbs. French brandy

Cream first 3 ingredients until soft as thick cream. Beat egg yolks until thick. Alternate mixing sugar, flour, and egg yolks into creamed butter. Beat well. Mix in brandy. Gently fold in well-beaten egg whites until well-blended. Grease and dust with flour 10-inch tubed pan or two 9x5x3-inch loaf pans. Pour in batter and bake at 350° F. about 1 hour and 45 minutes.

One 10-inch tubed cake or 2 loaves

Mrs. Theodore Roosevelt's
INDIAN PUDDING

3 c. milk
½ c. yellow corn meal
¼ c. sugar
1 t. salt
1 t. ground cinnamon
½ t. ground ginger
1 egg, well beaten
½ c. light molasses
2 tbs. butter
1 c. cold milk

Scald 3 c. milk in a double boiler. Stirring constantly, blend scalded milk into a mixture of the next 5 ingredients. Vigorously stir some of this mixture into a blend of beaten egg and molasses. Stir this blend into hot corn meal mixture. Stirring constantly, cook over boiling water until very thick (about 10 minutes). Beat in butter. Turn into buttered 1½ -qt. casserole. Pour cold milk over top. Bake at 300° F. for 2 hours, or until browned. Serve warm with heavy cream or ice cream.

About 6 servings

Carols

While Shepherds Watched Their Flocks

Favorite Carol of George Washington

Nahum Tate, 1652–1715

Arranged from George F. Handel, 1685–1759

We Three Kings of Orient Are

Favorite Carol of Abraham Lincoln

John H. Hopkins, 1857 John H. Hopkins, 1857

From *The International Book of Carols* edited by Walter Ehret and George K. Evans. Copyright © 1963, 1980 by Walter Ehret and George K. Evans. Reprinted by permission

O Come, All Ye Faithful

Favorite Carol of Dwight D. Eisenhower

J.F. Wade
Translation: Frederick Oakley, alt. 1841

J.F. Wade, ca 1740

2. *Cantet nunc Io! chorus angelorum;*
Cantet nunc aula caelestium:
Gloria, gloria, in excelsis Deo:
Venite adoremus, etc.

3. *Ergo qui natus die hodierna,*
Jesu, tibi sit gloria!
Patris aeterni Verbum caro factum:
Venite adoremus, etc.

2. Sing, choirs of angels, sing in exultation,
Sing, all ye citizens of heav'n above!
Glory to God, all glory in the highest!
O come, let us adore Him, etc.

3. Yea, Lord, we greet Thee, born this holy morning,
Jesus, to Thee be glory giv'n!
Word of the Father, now in flesh appearing:
O come, let us adore Him, etc.

Acknowledgments

Cover: © Jack Novak, SuperStock
2: © John Aikins, Pictor
6: © Lani Howe, Photri
7: © Alex Wong, Newsmakers/Getty Images
8: © Pictor
9: © Steven Gottlieb, Taxi/Getty Images
10: (Left) © John Aikins, Pictor
(Right) © A. Pierce Bounds, Pictor
11: © Rick Brady, Pictor
12: Franklin D. Roosevelt Library
13: AP/Wide World
15: © Everett C. Johnson
16: © Larry Downing, Reuters
17: © Larry Downing, Reuters/Corbis
18: (Left) The White House
(Right) © Diana Walker, Getty Images
19-23: The White House
24: The Newberry Library, Chicago
25: AP/Wide World
26: The Newberry Library, Chicago
27: (Top) © John Aikins, Pictor
(Bottom) The Newberry Library, Chicago
28-29: Corbis/Bettmann
30: Harry S. Truman Library
31: (Top) Dwight D. Eisenhower Library
(Bottom) National Museum of American History
32: (Left) Hulton Archive/Getty Images
(Right) John F. Kennedy Library
34: © Fred J. Maroon
36: © Lisa Berg
37-38: © Joan Marcus
39: National Museum of American History
40: © Andre Jenny, Alamy
41: © Regis Lefebure, Folio, Inc.
44: National Museum of American History
45: (Left) © Everett C. Johnson
(Right) Hulton Archive/Getty Images
46: Hulton Archive/Getty Images
47: © Linda Bartlett, Folio, Inc.
49: © Ron Goor, Bruce Coleman Inc.
50: The Shrine of the Immaculate Conception
51: © Everett C. Johnson
53: The National Shrine, Washington, D.C.
54: St. John's Church
55: © Mark Broffman
56: © Ron Goor, Bruce Coleman Inc.
57: The Newberry Library, Chicago
58: © Carol Highsmith
60: © John Aikins, Pictor
61: (Top) © Fred J. Maroon
(Bottom) © Julie Marcotte, Pictor
62: (Top) © Leslie Hendren, Folio Inc.
(Bottom) © Robert C. Schafer, Folio Inc.
63: © Mark Theissen, Corbis
64: © Carol Pratt

Recipe Cards: Eileen Mueller Neill*
Advent Calendar: © Richard Nowitz, National Geographic/Getty Images
Advent Calendar Illustrations: Eileen Mueller Neill*
All entries marked with an asterisk(*) denote illustrations created exclusively for World Book, Inc.